Protecting Your
Nest Egg

Fraud Protection for Senior
Citizens from Con Artists, Thieves
& Scams

Thank You

A special thank you to Visiting Angels, and to the administrative staff, caregivers and clients I've met and worked with through my Visiting Angels franchise.

Thank you to the Visiting Angels corporate staff for your encouragement and support, and to my fellow Visiting Angels franchise owners across the country and around the world.

If you or a loved one is in need of home care, check us out at www.visitingangels.com, or call 1-800-365-4189.

Protecting Your Nest Egg
Fraud Protection for Senior Citizens
from Con Artists, Thieves & Scams

Copyright 2014 Page Cole

Table of Contents

Foreword

Protecting Your Nest Egg: Fraud Protection for Senior Citizens from Con Artists, Thieves & Scams couldn't come at a better time! As an eldercare expert and daughter of aging parents I have seen and heard of many scams targeting older adults, unfortunately many too late to save the individual or couple from the damaging results!

We are all open to con artists and scams but as Page Cole points out, older adults are more vulnerable for the reasons he describes. I have been the victim of credit card fraud finding unknown and unapproved charges on my bank statement when my card was neither misplaced, lost, nor stolen. How the criminals got my information is still a mystery to me, but I was able to report and get my funds back quickly because of my diligent monitoring of my account through online banking. I consider myself street smart as a woman who grew up in the streets of Detroit, and try and keep up with the latest cons and scams to protect myself and my family, and to warn older adults and family caregivers when I can, but I wasn't even aware of the vast majority of scams Page Cole has so diligently researched and included in this book.

Many times I have warned my parents about not believing everything they see and hear because I have diverted them from being taken advantage of more than once. As most Mom's, my mother is very concerned about the autoimmune health problems that affect my sister and I and she is always looking for the "cure". Recently she called me and started to read a letter she received about this miracle cure product she was sure could help me, as it claimed. I asked her where she got this information and she said she received it in the mail. I asked her if she checked out the company online. She had not. I urged her to refrain from reading and believing claims like this without

"Googling" the company or product name. I took the name down and told her I'd check them out and call her back. I Googled the name of this product and the #2 listing on the first page was a Food and Drug Administration warning of the product and it's claims. They were supposedly shut down and stopped two years prior but obviously were still in the scam business as the letter my mom received was recent.

I can honestly say that my mom may have purchased and sent me this product in hopes it would help my daily struggles with Chronic Fatigue and Sjogren's Syndromes. I'm grateful she chose to discuss it with me first, but it's an example of how easily one can be scammed. Her concern for my sister and I overshadowed the red flags that should have been all over that letter. I reported the continued scam to the FDA in hopes they can stop these scammers for good!

I almost have to laugh about one of our older family members rescheduling a family reunion flight because they were sure the Publisher's Clearing House Prize Patrol was scheduled to make a home visit to dole out that million dollar prize on the day they were initially scheduled to fly, and they didn't want to miss their mega prize! It turned into a Jeff Foxworthy type of joke between my sister and me saying, "You know your elderly relative is gullible if they schedule their vacation around the Publisher's Clearing House prize day giveaway!" In truth, it's not funny at all because it just proves how easily older adults can get sucked in to believing everything they read or hear.

Many years ago when I worked as a home health and hospice nurse a patient of mine who'd had a significant stroke had a private caregiver her husband hired to help with her care. After a month or so of visiting her, her husband confided in me that the private caregiver talked them into getting a second mortgage on their home to buy her a truck because her vehicle broke down and she couldn't get to work. I was livid that these wonderful people had fallen prey to this woman and were now thousands of dollars in mortgage debt late in life when their house had been previously paid off. I notified their adult children who lived out of state, their primary physician and in turn they notified the authorities. Unfortunately it was too late to reverse this decision and the only recourse they had was to let the caregiver go. Even after she took advantage of them, they wanted to keep her because they liked her and didn't see what she did as a scam. As Page points out, it's embarrassing to admit, even to ourselves, that we've been duped by a con artist, or fallen prey to a scam.

I am very appreciative of the time and effort it took to write this book and not only did I learn from the information set forth, I will use it as the confirmation I need to warn my parents so they are not taken advantage of or scammed out of their hard earned money and/or assets. Even as an expert with 30 years in the field my parents are more apt to believe a virtual stranger than listening to my voice of experience and concern. Because I am personally aware of Page Cole's heart, passion, and integrity I can trust the purpose and information contained in *Protecting Your Nest Egg*. I met Page 8 years ago when we attended a homecare conference, and we quickly became friends when I saw the depth of his concern and commitment to the senior population.

As 78 million Baby Boomers age there are more and more individuals jumping into the field of aging and care. Many have one focus and that is to benefit financially without any real concern for older adults. Scams are at an all-time high and will continue to rise. Page has the background, stellar reputation, and has done the homework for you and me so we can better protect ourselves and our families with this comprehensive guide.

I implore children of aging parents to utilize the SCAM PREVENTION WORKSHEET and the SCAM RISK SURVEY, both great tools in understanding how much attention we need to pay to what is going on with our parent's and to educate ourselves and our parents on prevention before it's too late. If hundreds of intelligent younger, middle aged and older adults can fall prey to Bernie Madoff and lose their life savings in the biggest scheme in US history, we are all at least at some risk to become victims of the evil that preys on us all.

I am grateful and honored to share my thoughts on Page's book and my experience with Page as a colleague and dear friend. I share his hope that this book will protect the most vulnerable from those who are trying to hurt them.

Sincerely,

Angil Tarach-Ritchey RN, GCM

Angil Tarach-Ritchey RN, GCM is a highly respected national eldercare expert, speaker, consultant, and the best-selling and multi award winning author of Behind the Old Face: Aging in America and the Coming Elder Boom.
http://www.elderboom.org

Dedication

"To care for those who once cared for us is one of the highest honors." Tia Walker, *The Inspired Caregiver: Finding Joy While Caring for Those You Love*

Sift through the fondest memories of your heart. Walk slowly through visions of your past, and pause for moment. Pause at those moments of deep love, at those instances of greatest warmth and joy. If you're like most, many of those visions include elderly grandparents, sweet little old ladies at church or elderly teachers and neighbors.

Seniors hold a special place in our hearts and histories for a various reasons. For some it's because they came alongside us at a time in our life where we needed an encouraging word or a hand up, and they were there to offer it. For others, it was a word of wisdom at just the right time, and that wisdom changed our family, our faith in our selves or our futures. And for the rest of us, it may just be that a senior in our past was there for us when no one else was.

But something has happened in our culture. Where seniors once occupied a place of respect and honor, they have now become an easy mark to the thieves and scam artists. Rather than respect the position of dignity seniors have earned over the years, criminals take advantage of the weakened physical state, loneliness and susceptible state many of our elderly find themselves in. The end result for seniors is an empty bank account and a broken spirit.

So how do we keep this from happening? We educate. We inform. We guard our seniors from these scam artists by being aware and protective of their finances and their hearts.

I've been blessed to have seniors who've crossed my path over the years who encouraged me, invested in me and guided me when I really needed it most. My grandparents, my parents and in-laws are at the top of the list. This book is dedicated to their love and protection for me when I was younger.

To the seniors in churches where I've served in El Reno, Hydro, Sapulpa and Owasso, Oklahoma, who were patient and parental, who offered wisdom when it was timely & love most liberally, this book is dedicated to their investment in my life as well.

In my work with Visiting Angels, I've been blessed to meet seniors who were some of most amazing, kind and gentle spirits on the planet. In a time of their liveswhere their bodies and minds have been ravaged by the cruel ticks of the clock, they still find ways to bring hope and encouragement to the rest of us. They too are a source of my inspiration, and this book has been written to both protect and honor them. They are truly inspirational.

Protecting our seniors is not something we "can" do, or "should" do. We MUST protect them at all costs. Abraham J. Heschel once said, *"A test of a people is how it behaves toward the old. It is easy to love children. Even tyrants and dictators make a point of being fond of children. But the affection and care for the old, the incurable, the helpless are the true gold mines of a culture."*

Let it be said of our generation that we were faithful to protect and care for our seniors.

If you or a loved one needs assistance in living at home, then contact Visiting Angels Living Assistance Services at 800-365-4189, or check them out at www.visitingangels.com for an office location near you!

America's Choice in Homecare

Protecting Your Nest Egg

Fraud Protection for Senior Citizens from Con

Artists, Thieves & Scams

UNDERSTANDING WHY SENIORS ARE AT GREATER RISK

Crime knows no discrimination when it comes to conning people out of their hard earned cash.  **Melba had worked as a teacher for most of her life, and her husband Jim had spent his entire career in a manufacturing plant. Between their salaries they had been able to put aside a nice nest egg for their Golden Years of retirement. Suddenly that was all in jeopardy.**

Melba had been fooled by a kind sounding voice on the other end of the telephone. The sweet young man had reminded her of her own

grandson as he described a fresh new investment plan for seniors, and how it could double their portfolio in only a few years. All he needed to do was to set up the accounts, and once the investment fund was linked to their cash account, Melba and Jim could move as much or as little money into the new investment account. At least that's what he told her.

She was excited when Jim came in from playing golf, and wanted to show him the new financial tool she had signed them up for. As she logged on to their bank account online, she was stunned to see that one of their "nest egg" accounts had been totally emptied. As she stared blankly at the screen, she covered mouth with her hand, and her eyes brimmed with tears. "How could I have been so foolish?" she cried to her husband. "I trusted a complete stranger! What are we going to do?" This scene has repeated itself thousands of times over with seniors across the country.

Data from a recent survey, sponsored by the University of Waterloo, indicated that the percentage of victims of scams and fraud in an age group peaks in late middle age, and then declines as people get older. That being said, seniors as a group tend to be a greater target for many reasons. Among those reasons are:

Shame
Seniors tend to allow shame and embarrassment to keep them from sharing about their scam with family, friends or law enforcement;

Vulnerability
Seniors are more vulnerable than younger adults, especially if they have become widowed;

Passive
The elderly tend to be much less likely to try to fight back than median age or younger adults;

Sensory Issues

Since seniors are more likely to have trouble with their hearing or sight, they can be more easily fooled;

Mental Faculties

With age and the possible onset of various health conditions, their thought processes may not be as sharp. This is even more dangerous if the senior has experienced the onset of any form of dementia;

Affects of Aging

They are less able to protect themselves both physically and emotionally;

Danger of Injury

Injuries to the elderly are more likely to be very serious or life threatening;

Desperation

With limited or fixed incomes and a tough economy, many seniors level of desperation pushes them to take risks they might not normally take with their finances;

Detachment

It's easy for seniors to feel neglected or detached from busy family members; they become very receptive to the suggestions or direction of others who will pay them attention or spend time with them;

Technologically Disadvantaged

Seniors tend to be less technologically savvy, and are more like to be tricked with online scams.

Increased Assets

Seniors tend to have larger cash reserves and resources, making them a much higher priority as a target for scammers.

Sweepstakes & Contests

An AARP study noted that seniors place themselves at a greater risk for being a victim of fraud by doing seemingly innocent things like entering drawings, contests and sweepstakes for the promise of free trips, vacations or prizes; attending free seminars; sitting through time share or others sales pitch meetings; and reading and accepting junk mail offers.

WHY ARE THE ELDERLY LESS LIKELY TO REPORT SCAMS?

So why do seniors who have been scammed fail to immediately contact family and/or the authorities? Don't they want their money back? Aren't they interested in doling out justice to the liars who have taken advantage of them? Typically, seniors fail to report these kinds of scams to anyone. The reasons for this failure to respond vary.

Fear of Family Perception

More often than not, seniors tend to worry about what their family might do if they find out. Grown children can react or overreact by grossly limiting or even removing their parent's access to their own money. Although this may very well be in the senior's best interest, it can be both frightening and humiliating for the senior.

Self-Blame

Defrauded seniors also blame themselves for what happened. Remember, this senior has been a productive and thoughtful member of society. They've held down jobs, raised families and volunteered in their community. No one is more disappointed in them than they are themselves. They might even adopt the belief that they deserve what they got, for not paying more attention or being more discerning.

Pride

Personal pride may also play a part in their response to being scammed. Seniors may believe that they are smart enough or savvy enough to get their money back on their own without any assistance from others. As seniors age, their control of so much of the different areas can slip away- their health, driving ability, even finances.   For many this is a matter of life long pride. "I got myself into this pickle, so I can get myself out of it," is their mantra.

Scammers are Relatives

Sadly enough, many scammed seniors are related to or have a prior relationship with the person who scammed them. When it is a loved one, friend or business acquaintance that has scammed them, they may determine that the relationship is more

Seniors who have been scammed would rather face the fear of lost money than the retaliation of the scammer.

valuable to them than the assets are. In deference to keeping the relationship with a nephew, neighbor or friend, they will just keep quiet and take the loss.

Fear

Another reason seniors may stay silent about their loss is that they are afraid the person who scammed them might retaliate. This is a very real concern for seniors who have become feeble or dependent upon others for the most basic needs of life. They scenario is more likely the case when intimidation was a part of the initial scam. Seniors who have been scammed would rather face the fear of lost money than the retaliation of the scammer.

Uncertainty about Legal System

The prospect of going through the court system and dealing with lawyers, law enforcement and judges scares many people, and seniors are no different. Seniors face unknown or unrealistic fears about what new legal fees they might face. With investment schemes, there may even be concerns on the part of the senior that they themselves might have a legal problem.

Embarrassment

Don't forget, many seniors are totally

embarrassed about what has happened to them. This is by far the most prominent reason seniors fail to report scams and frauds. They can't believe that they were gullible enough to lose so much money. They certainly don't want others to look down on them or ridicule them for this failure, so instead they just stay silent.

Worry About Housing
If the victim is a resident of a nursing home, assisted living facility or retirement community, they may fear they would get kicked out of their home. Again, this may have been an intimidation tactic employed by an employee of the facility who scammed them, or simply a seed of fear planted in their mind by the scammer.

Ignorance

Believe it or not, some seniors are unaware that what happened to them was a crime. As strange as that may seem, some seniors may not understand the criminal nation of the fraud that has been committed against them.

Resignation to Failure

Finally, some will fail to report the crime simply because they are afraid that there aren't enough facts to prove they were scammed. No one goes into one of these situations believing or expecting that they are being scammed. With an attitude of trust, and feelings of excitement about this new endeavor, many times well-meaning and intelligent seniors may not be as focused on details and record keeping as they should be. As a result, there are verbal contracts, handshakes and gentlemen's agreements, rather than documented paperwork and legitimate contracts.

The AARP regularly studies issues related to seniors and fraud issues. Their studies reflect that many seniors who are telemarketing fraud victims don't understand that the sweet sounding young man who just called them could be planning on stealing their life savings.

The National Consumers League's National Fraud Information Center constantly monitors issues regarding scams and fraud across the country. They estimate that of all telemarketing fraud victims, nearly 1/3 of them are over 60 years old.

It's just not safe or prudent in this day and age to assume that anyone trying to "sell you up" or "sign you up" is honest. Quite the contrary is the case in many instances. Where seniors would like to believe that voice on the other end of the line belongs to a nice young man or woman simply trying to make an honest days' wage. If they are too pushy or seem to confrontational, seniors would tend to believe the best of them anyway. The nice young man on the phone might seem to "stretch the truth" just a bit; many will still err on the side of trust rather than caution.

Of course, the telemarketing industry has a large number of honest and trustworthy people working in it. Still, there are those wolves in sheep's clothing laying in wait for unsuspecting senior citizens, and without losing one bit of sleep, will bilk them out of hundreds or even thousands of dollars. Unlike a gun toting mugger in a dark alley, these thieves use a phone as their weapon of choice. It's simply too dangerous and too devastating to trust too

> *It's simply too dangerous and too devastating to trust too much.*

much.

Thousands... yes thousands of deceptive tele-marketing companies are open for business daily, according to the FBI. Beyond our borders, there are thousands more around the world who intentionally target U.S. residents from locations as close as Canada and as far away as Nigeria, India and Russia.

Given the global scope and the constant barrage of these kinds of financial assaults on seniors, help them out by suggesting educating and equipping them with the following suggestions.

CONVINCE SENIORS OF THEIR GENUINE RISK

Senior adults look at the world through a different perspective than many other generations. Theirs was a generation that freely gave strangers stranded on the roadside a ride, or invited complete strangers into their home for dinner.

Jerry and Louise have been enjoying their retirement for a few years now. They travel some, and each has finally been able to spend time on those hobbies that work and raising a family kept them from for years. Jerry had retired from a successful insurance practice, and Louise had been a cosmetologist for over 40 years. A lifetime of working directly with people on a daily basis caused them both to believe they were a good judge of character. When a friend mentioned a new investment opportunity regarding lakefront lot properties, they were sure they would be able to tell if this was the "real deal" or not.

The meeting with Steve, the salesman for Venture Adventure Properties, went better than Jerry and Louise had expected it to. The lots were reasonably priced, and by Steve's description, the lakeshore area two states away was a booming and developing area that would most certainly make their property appreciate greatly in value. They took the "virtual tour" via the video demonstration, and were able to secure their lot with a simple down payment of $20K on a $55K 2 acre lakefront lot.

A few days later they decided to take a quick road trip to see first-hand their new investment real estate. To their surprise, when they arrived at the lakefront lot they had "purchased", the property already had a home on it, and all of it rightfully and legally belonged to that owner.

Repeated calls to Steve went unanswered, and the office complex where they'd met was now empty. They had been scammed.

Just as Jerry and Louise believed they were "too smart" to be taken advantage of, all seniors need to be educated that the world has changed, and that these scammers are in fact criminals. When they understand the criminal nature of what could happen to them, they may be more likely to hang up the phone and either call their family or call the police.

Our goal is not only to protect those we love, but to encourage them to speak up and protect others by raising awareness of the scams, and arresting and punishing those who perpetrate them.

HELP THEM UNDERSTAND THEIR VULNERABILITY

Seniors haven't always been old... and they haven't always been as vulnerable as they are now. They need to be educated in a way that helps them become aware and guarded, while at the same time maintaining their integrity and self-esteem. Many believe that it's only the lonely, isolated or foolish seniors that fall prey to scams. Nothing could be further from the truth.

If it sounds unbelievable, easy and profitable, it's safer to just stop at the word "unbelievable."

Retired teachers, physicians and a variety of well informed and educated professionals fall prey to the wiles of scam artists every day. AARP research reveals that it is many of these typical older victims are successful people who are simply tempted by allure of phony promises of amazing deals to grow their retirement "nest eggs." Scammers and unscrupulous telemarketers and con artists take full advantage of that. If it sounds unbelievable, easy and profitable, it's safer to just stop at the word "unbelievable."

We all want to believe that dreams can come true! We all hope someday we will get that call from Publisher's Clearing House, or see our stock choices take off overnight! Many seniors have worked hard, & it's easy to be convinced that their day has come. Family members are shocked when seniors react with frustration or anger if their optimistic response to a scam is questioned.

Seniors come from a generation where courtesy is always in style. Many seniors would NEVER consider hanging up on someone; they believe even strangers deserve their courtesy.

Scammers know this, and manipulate the good will and traditional heart of the Greatest Generation & Baby Boomers to their advantage.

Remind them that it's hard to discern who's really honest. Building a good relationship, creating an atmosphere of urgency, building excitement, building a sense of "need" in the senior- these are the tactics of both great salespeople and criminal shysters as well.

Warn them that the power of consistent pressure is overwhelming. Just check the mailbox of the typical senior. It is FULL of junk mail offering deals on property for sale, offers to work from home and get rich, and "add to your nest egg" offers. The numbers of scams thrown at seniors is mind boggling.

Discourage immediate trust from being the natural reaction. Giving someone the benefit of the doubt is the normal reaction for most seniors. They sound nice, they seem nice, so the person on the other side of the phone must BE nice, or so they believe.

RECOGNIZING THE WARNING SIGNS OF FRAUD

So how do you help seniors be aware of the signal fires of fraud? How can we equip them to spot the tell tail markers of typical scammers? Here are a few suggestions. Look Out For:

Refusal to Stop Calling

Be concerned if the caller refuses to stop calling after someone asks not to be called again. People truly working on commission in sales will not chase after cold leads. If someone continues to pursue them after being rebuffed, it's a danger sign that the motives of the caller may be dishonorable or even criminal.

Demand to Pay

Be concerned if there is a request or demand to purchase or pay something to enter a contest, collect a prize, or even the suggestion that your odds might increase if you spend some money. Not only is it dishonest, it's illegal.

Gerald picked up his mail on his way in from the grocery store. An interesting envelope with the label "You're A Winner" had his name across the front of it. As he read the enclosed letter, it informed him that he had won a trip to Miami, and that to claim his prize he simply needed to call the highlighted number, and pay a processing fee to receive his vouchers for a five day vacation on the beach. Gerald had seen other friends go down this road though, and he wasn't going to be taken in. He called and reported the information to the BBB and to his local police, and then chunked the letter in the trash.

There is nothing inherently wrong with

contests or sweepstakes. Many seniors enjoy entering these on a regular basis. The number one danger sign is the request for money. RUN, RUN, RUN AWAY!

Promise of Easy Money

Be concerned if the promise to win money or prizes, make easy money with little or no effort, or borrow money for nothing is the pitch. Even the Publishers Clearing House Sweepstakes requires you to complete an entry form! Truly, you can't expect to get something for nothing, or even next to nothing. One easy tool to discern whether a deal is a scam or not is simply to ask, "Is this designed to appeal to my greed, or to my business sense?" If it's the "easy money" deal, that's a lure to draw you in. Don't buy the lie.

Requests for Account Numbers

Be concerned if someone requests your bank account number, Social Security Number or credit card number. You should never ever, not ever, no never give out your bank account number, Social Security number or credit card you don't know and trust.

> _Never, ever, not ever, no never give out your bank account number, Social Security number or credit card._

The only exceptions to this rule would be that you are absolutely certain of the person asking for it. Obviously we give out this information at the Emergency Room or when applying for a loan. But much greater discretion should be used when doing ANYTHING on the internet.

Not only that, when one of your credit card companies or banks contacts you about your account, it's always a good idea to hang up and contact them back directly. Scammers can mask their telephone number on your caller ID to make it look like they are your mortgage company or your credit card vendor. Hang up and call them back using the number on the paperwork you've received directly from them.

Pressed for Immediate Response

Be concerned if you are pressed for an immediate response or a fast response. Criminals don't want you to have time to think about it, or to check with a loved one. Their goal is to get any money, get it quickly, and get away. If you are being pressed for an immediate answer, purchase or decision, simply hang up or walk away.

Scare Tactics

Be concerned if the caller or salesperson is using scare tactics to push you into a decision to buy or commit to spend money. Refer back to the last point. You don't owe ANYONE an immediate answer, so cut it off, walk away and don't look back!

Requests to Wire Money

Be concerned if someone asks you to wire money, send a gift card, use a courier or put money on a "money card" and send that as payment. This is the most obvious sign that you are being scammed.

Once you have sent the gift card, money card or wired the money, it's gone for good. Legitimate businesses will take standard forms of payment, and not require jumping through strange financial hoops like money cards or wiring funds.

Upfront Fees Expected

Be concerned if someone asks for an upfront fee to get a loan, guarantee a loan, or even to imply that a loan will be made. They can't promise that, and it's illegal for them to do so. In fact, you might watch their reaction when you tell them that requiring any fees paid up front for a loan is illegal. When you see defensiveness or anger, you'll know that the scammer realizes he's just been caught, and he's looking for a way out!

> _...Scammers aren't committed to getting big money, they just want any money they can get..._

No Information Provided

Be concerned if someone is unwilling or reticent about sending you written information about something before you buy it.

Legitimate purchases or investments always come with some kind of documentation. You should be able to cross reference this information with the local Better Business Bureau, as well as do your own research on the internet about the company and/or the opportunity.

Payment for Information Alone

Be concerned about anyone who wants even a minimal payment from you before getting the details about the offer or opportunity. Remember, many scammers aren't committed to getting big money; they just want any money they can get and get away with.

Better to lose out on a legitimate opportunity while you were checking it out, than to give away your hard earned cash to a sneaky criminal, and then have nothing to show for it but embarrassment.

SIGNALS SENIORS ARE VICTIMS OR AT GREAT RISK

The following signals may alert loved ones and friends that they may have already fallen pray to a scam.   Here are the top ten ways you can Pay Attention and protect yourself or your loved ones! Pay Attention to these signals!

Large or Increasing Subscriptions
PAY ATTENTION if you see a large number of magazine or book club subscriptions. This could be a warning that they are looking for the "quick, easy money". Many scammers use a "legitimate" front to build a trust relationship with seniors before taking advantage of them.

Increase in Incoming Phone Calls
PAY ATTENTION to an increase in the number of incoming phone calls. If the senior has seen a pick-up in number of phone calls regarding

donations to charity or touting special offers, they may be the target of one or more scammers. If you have access to check the phone bill occasionally, or simply pick up on this by spending more time with the senior, you might save them from tons of financial heartache down the road. Scammers count on no one paying attention.

Struggling to Pay Normal Bills

PAY ATTENTION if you become aware that they are struggling to pay their normal bills, buy gasoline and food or pay their utilities. This is a warning signal that they may have

> _Scammers count on no one paying attention._

used funds set aside for necessities in other ways, and may have actually lost important living expenses money to scammers. You will also want to take notice if a senior who has never needed to borrow money is suddenly asking for a quick, short term loan.

Obvious or Suspected Fraudulent Charges
PAY ATTENTION by taking immediate action if you become aware of potential fraud. Cancel credit cards or close bank accounts if you feel like they have or may have been compromised by scammers or thieves. Especially be concerned if the senior has used their debit card to purchase something expensive. Whereas most credit card companies have some measure of fraud protection built into them, once the money is gone from a checking or savings account through the use of a debit card, it is gone for good.

Odd New Products
PAY ATTENTION if you notice odd new products around the home. Things such as beauty products, jewelry, health/nutritional aides or weight loss products can be hints that something

is wrong. Also, notice if they have trinket prizes that were purchased with hopes to win something larger or more valuable. Con artists will take advantage of seniors by luring them in with "instant wins" of smaller items, with the hope of scoring the big prize later. The only problem is that there is never any big prize later, only a discouraged senior and an empty bank account.

Increased Sweepstake/Contest Mail

PAY ATTENTION if the senior has seen an increase in sweepstakes, prize & contest mail and email. Mail and sweepstakes fraud are one of the easiest way these criminals take advantage of seniors! Mailing and phone number lists are for sale all across the internet with the information for people who have a track record of purchasing things through the mail, and for participating in contests/sweepstakes. If the name of you or a loved one is on one of the lists, you can be sure it's on many of these lists. The unscrupulous people who purchase this information are interested in one thing only... taking someone else's hard earned money for them.

Financial Recovery Specialists

PAY ATTENTION if you become aware that "financial recovery specialists" are contacting the senior. If they are contacted by individuals or companies promising to recover money lost to fraud, especially if they want to charge a 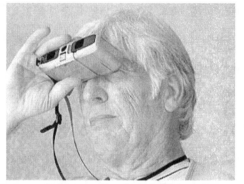 fee for this service, may actually be scammers themselves. These individuals make it sound so simple. Simply give them your SSN and your bank account number, and they will recover any bad debts owed to you, or even tax refunds or inheritances you did know about! However, what they do instead is open new accounts and lines of credit using the name of the person whose information they now have, and use that to borrow money or open credit cards they can abuse. What they leave in their wake is the destroyed credit of their innocent victim.

Strange or Repetitive Payments

PAY ATTENTION if you become aware that they have started making consistent and repetitive payments to strange companies. It's especially dangerous if those companies are located out of state or out of country. Be very cautious about phone calls that have unusual 2 digit numbers at the beginning- these are international calls, and once your money or information has crossed the borders of the USA, it's gone for good. In some foreign countries it is a badge of honor to steal, but especially to steal from Americans.

Tension between Senior & Family/Friend

PAY ATTENTION if you sense tension between a senior and either a friend or family member regarding finances. It could be that a loved one has actually preyed on the senior and abused the relationship for financial gain. Dig for details immediately and without reservation put a stop to any money or cash transfers that have been hidden or seem improper. Don't hesitate to bring in other family members or law enforcement if you believe something illegal has taken place. Even those we should be able to trust the most can take advantage of loved ones. Money issues among family members should be transparent and documented to avoid conflict.

Scammers Repeatedly Abuse Phone

PAY ATTENTION by changing the phone number if scammers repeatedly contact the senior, or won't stop calling back. In addition, don't hesitate to contact the authorities and turn the number in to them for harassment and potential elder abuse.   Doing so may protect other seniors in the area from being scammed, or assist law enforcement in apprehending the criminals and possibly recovering any lost assets.

> *Money issues among family members should be transparent and documented to avoid conflict.*

LIMITING SCAMMERS ACCESS TO SENIORS

Educate seniors with tips on reducing the onslaught of unsolicited junk mail pieces and dinner time phone calls from telemarketers.

IT'S IMPORTANT TO KNOW HOW TO AVOID "MAKING THE LIST".

"Mom, what are all of these sweepstakes forms sitting on your dining room table," Bob asked. "Oh, several of my friends have won prizes lately by entering contests! I

> *You don't owe it to any caller to implicitly trust that what they are telling you is in fact the truth.*

thought to myself 'someone has to win, it might as well be me!'".

What Bob's mother wasn't aware of was that one of the primary tasks of these kinds of contests is not the marketing aspect of any

67

product, but the task of gathering the names and contact information of unwitting seniors into a list, so that information could be sold time and time again. Seniors may not understand that by filling out the sweepstakes and contest entries, both hard copies and online, can land them on lists as potential suckers. Demand that companies you do business with protect and not share your information with anyone for any reason. Know your rights from the list below.

You Have Rights To Be Taken Off Their Lists.

Federal law dictates that you can order a telemarketer not to call you ever again. Simply go to the website www.ftc.gov/donotcall or call 1-888-382-1222 to put your numbers on the list. You may also put your cell phone on the list. Enforcement in these areas is fairly lax, but don't let that stop you from registering and making the call to the police. Many of these criminals will simply take your name off the list if you confront them because they don't want even a small chance of the police catching on to what they are doing.

Know Exactly Who You're Doing Business With.

Unfamiliar companies, charities and online businesses should be screened by taking advantage of the Better Business Bureau and any other local or state consumer protection agencies. Many times a simple Google Search will provide information about companies you are unsure of.

Although some criminals are very creative, many would fall into the "not the sharpest knife in the drawer" category. Some of these scammers move from one part of the country to another, and are simply too lazy to change their methods or name, but simply set up shop in a new region. Doing a minimal amount of online research may result in tons of savings and heartache.

Know How To Screen Your Calls.

You can use voice mail, an answering machine, Caller ID or phone services to screen your calls if you feel you are being harassed. One important note, however, is that software exists that allows the caller to put whatever name and phone number he or she wants to appear on your Caller ID. Since that technology is abused to take advantage of unwary seniors, it's always smart to ask for the name of the company, and see if you can get their main phone number through the phone book or through calling 411 Information, and then calling them back on that legitimate number.

If someone calls telling you they represent one of your current credit cards or other accounts, tell them you will call them back on their advertised numbers. If the caller becomes belligerent or confrontational with that approach, you can be certain that they are definitely a phony. You don't owe it to any caller to implicitly trust that what they are telling you is in fact the truth.

Have a Plan for Dealing with Telemarketers

Make a list of the questions you would want to ask before the phone ever rings. Be direct and courteous, but exercise your right to hang up if they are  unwilling to answer your questions or you sense something is off.

Questions you might ask are: "Where did you get my name and phone information?" or "Did you know that my name is on the National 'Do Not Call' list, and that this call is being recorded?" You could also ask, "Can I speak to your supervisor?", or "Would you please take me off of your list immediately? By the way, what was your name again?" Last but not least, my favorite question of all is, "I don't really have time to visit right now, but I would like to talk to you about this later? Can I have your home number so I can call you later? What? You don't want a stranger calling you at home? ME NEITHER!", and then hang up!

Data Collection is Big Business about You

Businesses have their own version of Caller ID, the Automatic Number Identification (ANI). This allows the company to quickly access your information if you have an account with the company, and retrieve your records and vital information quickly. That being said, some companies will abuse the ANI and use it for marketing purposes. It's your right to question what info is being collected.   You also have a right to tell the company that you don't want to be put on a marketing list.

Believe it or not, here are some of the pieces of information that are gathered on individuals, and then sold across thousands of different lists:

- ➢ Social Security Number
- ➢ Shopping preferences
- ➢ Health information, including diet type, allergies, arthritis, incontinence/bladder problems, diabetes, hearing loss, prostate problems, and visual impairment, birth defects
- ➢ Marital status
- ➢ Financial situation (solvency, creditworthiness, loan amounts, credit cards)
- ➢ Date of Birth
- ➢ Sex
- ➢ Age
- ➢ Household income
- ➢ Race and ethnicity
- ➢ Geography
- ➢ Physical characteristics, such as height and weight
- ➢ Household occupants (whether an individual has children)
- ➢ Telephone number
- ➢ Utility usage (electric or gas usage, telephone usage, cable or satellite usage, Internet subscription, cellular phone usage)

- Magazine subscriptions
- Occupation
- Level of education
- Likelihood to respond to "money-making opportunities"
- Congressional district
- Size of clothes worn
- Habits (smoking)
- Arrest records
- Lifestyle preferences
- Hobbies (whether and what the individual collects)
- Religion (affiliation and denomination)
- Homeownership
- Characteristics of residence (size, number of bedrooms and bathrooms, sale price, rent and mortgage payments)
- Type of automobile owned
- Characteristics of automobile owned (year, make, value, fuel type, number of cylinders, presence of vanity or special membership plates)
- Whether the individual responds to direct mail solicitations
- Contributions to political, religious, and charitable groups
- Membership in book, video, tape, and compact disk clubs
- Mail order purchases and type
- Product ownership (beeper, contact lenses, electronics, fitness equipment, recreational equipment)

- Pet ownership and type
- Interests (including gambling, arts, antiques, astrology)
- Book preferences
- Music preferences
- "Socialites"

One major profiling company actually has individuals classified in various identifiable groups. That list includes:

- "Elite Suburbs" (Blue Blood Estates, Winner's Circle, Executive Suites, Pools & Patios, Kids & Cul-de-Sacs).
- "Urban Uptown" (Urban Gold Coast, Money & Brains, Young Literati, American Dreams, Bohemian Mix).
- "2nd City Society" (Second City Elite, Upward Bound, Gray Power).
- "Landed Gentry" (Country Squires, God's Country, Big Fish Small Pond, Greenbelt Families).
- "Affluentials" (Young Influentials, New Empty Nests, Boomers & Babies, Suburban Sprawl, Blue-Chip Blues)
- "Inner Suburbs" (Upstarts & Seniors, New Beginnings, Mobility Blues, Gray Collars).

- ➤ "Urban Midscale" (Urban Achievers, Big City Blend, Old Yankee Rows, Mid-City Mix, Latino America).
- ➤ "2nd City Center" (Middleburg Managers, Boomtown Singles, Starter Families, Sunset City Blues, Towns & Gowns).
- ➤ "Exurban Blues" (New Homesteaders, Middle America, Red White and Blues, Military Quarters).
- ➤ "Country Families" (Big Sky Families, New Eco-topia, River City USA, Shotguns and Pickups).
- ➤ "Urban Cores" (Single City Blues, Hispanic Mix, Inner Cities).
- ➤ "2nd City Blues" (Smalltown Downtown, Hometown Retired, Family Scramble, Southside City).
- ➤ "Working Towns" (Golden Ponds, Rural Industria, Norma Rae-ville, Mines and Mills).
- ➤ "Heartlanders" (Agri-Business, Grain Belt).
- ➤ "Rustic Living" (Blue Highways, Rustic Elders, Back Country Folks, Scrub Pine Flats, Hard Scrabble).

The names and information on these lists, names like YOURS and YOUR LOVED ONE, can sell for as little as $65 per thousand names. It's easy to see why scammers would want to purchase the information of target groups that fit the mold of their "perfect mark".

Scams Will Only Stop When Victims Step Up

If you or a senior know of a scam or fraud has or is taking place, then report it to the National Fraud Information Center, 800-876-7060, M-F, 9 am to 5 pm, or at www.fraud.org. That information will be transmitted to law enforcement agencies. (Copied from www.fraud.org)

Scam artists love to target the elderly. Seniors can easily fall victim to scams that prey on their emotions in an effort to drain their bank account. Here's how to protect yourself!

Seniors are often prime targets for scam artists. Older adults might not realize they have been scammed, or don't speak up because they are ashamed of being "suckered" by someone out to get their money. Some are afraid to report the scam, feeling it might be a sign of mental incompetence. But scams are very common, and even the smartest people can get pulled in. The next section highlights a few of the more popular scams that target the elderly.

CURRENT & COMMON SCAMS

There are a number of scams aimed at taking advantage of seniors that are among the most common scams currently working the senior circuit.

Home Remodels or Home/Auto Repairs

These scams can involve driveway repair, roof and guttering repair, or any number of housing remodels. A newer version of this scam involves phony roof repairmen moving through towns that have suffered major wind, hail or storm damage, and signing quick inexpensive contracts for repair. After the initial down payment is made, the repairmen do a quick substandard repair job and get their final payment, or they simply vanish without ever lifting a finger. Either way, the remodel isn't done or done well, and the individual has been scammed. Tips to help protect seniors from home repair scams include:

- ➤ Never let a repairman pressure you into making a quick or immediate decision about hiring them or doing a specific repair;

- ➤ Before you hire any contractor, check him out using a service like AngiesList.com or the Better Business Bureau;

- ➤ If an uninvited contractor shows up and offers or pressures to make an inspection or just "take a look around", refuse and contact the police;

- ➤ If using a contractor for large remodels or construction jobs, require that he obtain mechanic's lien waivers from any subcontractors or suppliers;

➢ **Get a least bids from at least three contractors if the job is in excess of $500;**

➢ **Settle for nothing less than a signed contract from any contractor, describing when the job will be started and completed, and especially the quality and types of materials. Include a partial payment schedule in the contract, with certain benchmarks to be met before payment is made.**

Dishonest auto mechanics may falsely inform customers that certain repairs are needed, or they may bill for services or repairs that were not requested or were not completed.

Grandparent Scam

A grandparent gets a call or e-mail from someone claiming to be a grandchild in trouble abroad. For instance, the scammer may claim "I've been arrested in Mexico, and I need money wired quickly to pay my bail. And oh by the way, don't tell my mom or dad because they'll only get upset!" The call is fraudulent impersonation, the name of the grandchild typically obtained from social media postings, and any money wired out of the country is gone forever. Nearly always the scammer encourages their grandparent to either wire money or put it on a money card of some kind and send it via overnight delivery.

Romance Scam

The traditional romance scam has the scammer working to build a long distance relationship with an individual, with a long term goal of exploiting that relationship for financial gain. Once trust is built, then the scammer uses a false crisis to extract money from their victim.

 This scam has now moved into the Internet dating sites. The con actively cultivates a romantic relationship which often involves promises of marriage. However, after some time it becomes evident that this Internet "sweetheart" is stuck in his or her home country or a third country, or in a distant city, or in jail; whatever the crisis, he or she is lacking the money to leave and thus unable to be united with the mark. The scam then becomes an advance-fee fraud or a check fraud.

A wide variety of reasons can be offered for the trickster's lack of cash, but rather than just borrow the money from the victim (advance fee fraud), the con-person normally declares that he has checks which the victim can cash on his behalf and remit the money via a non-reversible transfer service to help facilitate the trip. Of course, the checks are forged or stolen and the con-person never makes the trip: the hapless victim ends up with a large debt and an aching heart. This scam can be seen in the movie Nights of Cabiria.

Inheritance from Estate of a Wealthy Individual

You receive an email or a letter from a legal firm, informing you that a very wealthy individual has died, and that you have the ability to benefit from their death. You have the opportunity to claim your share of the estate, simply by providing your bank account number, name of your bank, etc. so that they can transfer millions of dollars into your account. This is necessary because they need a legal U.S. resident to be able to legally bring this money into the United States. They will allow you to keep a significant portion of these assets for assisting them with this transfer of funds into an American bank.

Of course, if someone makes the bad choice to provide their banking and other personal information, they will not only find their own bank account wiped clean, but they run the risk of having their identity stolen.

Duplicate Facebook Page Scam
These hackers very simply create a duplicate but phony Facebook page of an existing individual, and then use that page to scam the friends of the individual who they are pretending to be. This can be done by creating a phony crisis, such as an emergency health need

or family crisis, and asking for money to aid their situation.

This scam can also be used as a launch point to point people towards Ponzi Schemes, phony websites or to invite people to click a hyperlink to send the mark to an important website, only to have their identity stolen with keystroke copying software or other spyware.

Debt or Tax Collectors Scam

Many seniors have fallen victim the phony debt collector. This comes in many forms. It could be a call about an overdrawn bank account, a past due credit card, or even someone representing the state or federal government claiming that taxes haven't been paid. These scammers tend to be very confrontational and intimidating, making strong threats about everything from home foreclosure to jail time.

Work from Home Scam

With the economic troubles in our country many seniors struggle to maintain their standard of living. In the face of a bad economy, many seniors are looking for part time jobs to make ends meet. Faced with a very competitive job market, the opportunity to work from their own home is very appealing to seniors. Scammers seize this opportunity and offer non-existent work from home jobs with ridiculously high incomes. The senior simply needs to send a "start up" fee, or "registration" fee to receive their work packet, accreditation or whatever lie the scammer can come up with to entice their mark to send them money.

Health Insurance and Prescription Drug Scams

There are several types of health insurance fraud, and many of the schemes target those on Medicare or Medicaid. Bogus tests might be offered at shopping centers or health clubs and then billed to insurance, or prescription drugs ordered over the Internet might not be medication at all--you wind up paying the full amount for nothing more than a placebo.

Do Not Call Scams

The National Do Not Call Registry (U.S.) or the National Do Not Call List (Canada) offer  consumers a free way to reduce telemarketing calls. Scammers call anyway, of course, and they've even found a way to scam consumers by pretending to be a government official calling to sign you up or confirming your previous participation on the Dot Not call list! In one variation, scammers ask for personal information, such as your name, address and Social Security/Social Insurance number. In another, scammers try to charge a fee to join the registry. Either way, just hang up. These services are free, but sharing personal information with a scammer could cost you a lot.

Affordable Care Act Scam

Scammers have been successful using the Affordable Care Act ("Obamacare"), as a tool to trick seniors into sharing their most valuable personal information. These thieves claim to be from the government and claim the victim needs a new insurance or Medicare card because of Obamacare. One small catch, though... before the card can be mailed, the "agent" needs to collect personal information. They may already have a few pieces of personal information that convinces the victim that the person on the other end of the line is legitimate. Once they've retrieved all the information they want, there is nothing to stop them from opening bank accounts & credit cards in the name of the victim.

Cashier's Check Scams

This scam happens when the ultimate victim is advertising something for sale on the internet. A supposed "buyer," makes contact with the seller about buying the item. The scammer informs the seller that he needs to make the purchase using a cashier's check issued from a bank in the United States. The buyer contacts the seller later, and explains that he either will be sending a check for more than the purchase price, or that he mistakenly sent a check for too much money. The seller asks the seller to wire the "balance" back immediately.

Innocently enough, the seller deposits the cashier's check in their bank account, and quickly sends the "overpayment" to the buyer. Here's the problem. Federal banking law in the United States requires the customer's bank to make those funds available to its customer on the first business day after the funds are deposited. The seller is then able to withdraw & send the "overpayment" before the check makes its back to the bank that supposedly issued it. Many times that can take as long as 7 to 10 days.

When the bank of origin denies the check (since they never issued it) it will be sent back to the seller's bank, which will then require reimbursement from the seller. If the check is ultimately dishonored, the seller becomes obligated to pay the amount due on the check.

The bank whose name appears on the counterfeit check has no responsibility to honor it.

So how should one respond if offered payment with a cashier's check?

- ➢ Call the bank that issued the cashier's check when you receive it.

- ➢ Never accept a cashier's check for a larger amount than the purchase price.

- ➢ Verify the following information when talking with the bank that supposedly issued the cashier's check: amount of check, check number, & the name of the person to whom the check was issued.

- ➢ Never send the goods being sold until the check has cleared the bank it was issued from.

➤ Don't complete the exchange if a buyer gives you a check on the weekend or when banks are closed, and the check cannot be verified right away.

➤ Look up the phone number to the issuing bank yourself. Don't trust any contact information the buyer gives you.

Funeral and Cemetery Fraud

Some funeral homes may try to charge for services that are not required. For instance, purchasing a casket or being embalmed are not requirements for direct cremation, but some funeral homes may try to convince you that they are. Disreputable cemeteries may try to sell plots that are already taken and pocket your pre-paid money before you learn of the deception.

Car Ads

It sounds like a great job! "Get Paid Just for Driving Around" sounds like the perfect job for a senior. A company is offering $400 to $500 per week to simply drive your car around with their logo on your car. The company sends the unsuspecting mark a check. The victim then is instructed to deposit in their account and then wire a partial payment to a graphic designer. The "designer" will create a graphic wrap custom designed to fit the car of the senior. In a week to 10 days, the check bounces & the graphic designer the senior sent a check to has disappeared. The poor victim is out the money they wired to the designer is gone... for good.

Telemarketing Scams

Phone calls that promise luxurious vacations, deep discounts on medical supplies, or large prizes are probably scams. These cons are dedicated to getting financial information, such as a credit card number or bank account number. Once they have it, they can steal large amounts of money and claim it was legitimate.

Empty Promises of Cures/ Anti-aging Products

Products that promise cures for serious medical problems might be the most unsavory scams of all. They prey on vulnerability and hope, ensuring something that is simply too good to be true. If a "secret formula" seems the answer to all your problems, it is probably a well-laid scam.

Another take on this scam revolves around pills, shots, creams and other products that either slow or reverse the aging process. The lure of vanishing wrinkles and revitalized health are sometimes too much of a temptation for the senior to refuse, and before long their bank account is empty, and they've simply added more stress, wrinkles and worry lines.

Social Security Rip-off

Seniors may not even see this one coming. Some thieves have become experts in finding ways to steal the personal information from seniors, including their Social Security number. Then they contact the contact the Social Security Administration to change the payment routing information to the thieves' own bank accounts or prepaid debit cards.

Investment Scams

Seniors who have saved well over the years might find their nest egg depleted by investment scams. If high returns are "guaranteed" or you have to pay a fee up-front to obtain information, beware! A hallmark of investment schemes is the "proof" of individuals who have earned great dividends--but as the scheme plays out, those who are snared later wind up losing money...

Because many seniors live on fixed incomes, they often want to increase the value of their estate and ensure they have sufficient funds to meet basic needs. In investment scams, offenders persuade the elderly to invest in precious gems, real estate, annuities, or stocks and bonds by promising unrealistically high rates of return. The investments often consist of fake gemstones, uninhabitable property, or shares in a nonexistent or unprofitable company.

Prizes and Sweepstakes

These frauds generally involve informing the victim that he or she could win, or has already won, a "valuable" prize or a lot of money. The victim is required to send in money to cover taxes, shipping, or processing fees. The prize may never be delivered or, if so, is usually costume jewelry or cheap electronic equipment worth less than the money paid to retrieve it.

Charity Contributions

Playing on some seniors' desire to help others, offenders solicit donations to nonexistent charities or religious organizations, often using sweepstakes or raffles to do so.

Discount Prescription Card

Scammers call seniors and offer them a membership card to buy prescription drugs at 50 percent off. But there's a catch: These criminals charge a "nominal $200 "membership fee" to join the discount club, along with seniors' credit card numbers to debit a small monthly fee. Typically the drugs never show up as promised, or the "medicine" is actually a generic herbal replacement.

Seniors simply need to cynical of "too good to be true" offers. Encourage seniors to check with their state's program for low-income health insurance (often called a state health insurance program, or SHIP). These agencies maintain a list of reputable discount programs.

Jury Duty Scam

To make this threat seem real, the caller ID identifies the caller as that of the local sheriff. Victims are told they must pay a fine to avoid arrest. They aggressively confront the senior and accuse them of missing jury duty, and tell them that a warrant has been issued for their arrest. Fines are in the hundreds, sometimes, thousands of dollars. The payment is requested through Western Union, Green Dot prepaid card, or similar form of untraceable currency exchange. Many times people who live in nursing homes or assisted living facilities are targeted by this scam.

Credit Card Company Fraud

This scammer often calls late in the evening, pretending to be from the senior's credit card company. Because the thief has someone obtained the last 4 numbers of the senior's credit card (through deception or various other means), he gains their trust and belief when he shares those numbers with them. His story is that he is simply checking on a possible fraudulent purchase. When the senior refutes the charge, the caller offers to reverse the charge for them. To do so, he simply needs the full credit card number, and the three- or four-digit verification code on the back of his or her credit card.

Loans and Mortgages

Seniors may experience cash flow shortages in the face of needed medical care or home repairs. Predatory lenders may provide loans with exorbitant interest rates, hidden fees, and repayment schedules far exceeding the elderly persons' means, often at the risk of their home, which has been used as collateral.

Health, Funeral, and Life Insurance

Many seniors are concerned about having the funds to pay for needed medical care or a proper burial, or to bequeath to loved ones upon death. Unscrupulous salespeople take advantage of these concerns by selling the elderly policies that duplicate existing coverage, do not provide the coverage promised, or are altogether bogus.

Health Remedies

The elderly often have health problems that require treatment. Preying on this vulnerability, offenders market a number of ineffective remedies, promising "miracle cures." Unfortunately, given this false hope, many seniors delay needed treatment, and their health deteriorates further.

Close Contact I.O.U.

Relatives, neighbors, employees and close friends can easily persuade seniors to loan them money, and will even give them an I.O.U. in writing, even though they have no plans to ever pay them back. Understand that many seniors are starving for companionship and loan money because they're lonely and believe the loan will buy the affection and time of others. They worry what the person requesting the loan will do if they refuse. The senior doesn't want to seem cheap, unfeeling or selfish. They tell themselves: "I won't even miss the money... I'm not using it. It's not that much, and besides, I know they'll pay me back. Make no mistakes, this IS a crime, and if you know this is happening, it should be reported.

Phony CPR Training

For many seniors, health issues are the top priority on their list. They look for opportunities to improve their own health, as well as protect the health and welfare of their loved ones. Unscrupulous scammers will charge participants for phony CPR training classes, promising education about life saving skills and the accompanying certifications for the training. Instead, what they actually receive is a poor excuse for training, and no valid certifications.

Identity Theft

Identity theft costs millions of dollars to thousands of citizens and businesses to identity theft. Identity theft is defined as the unauthorized use of personal identifying and financial information for the purpose of stealing money and good credit.

In a 2003 survey released by the Federal Trade Commission (FTC), the results that nearly 10 million Americans had been victims of identity theft in one year. The cost of these crimes to victims amounted to $5 billion and the cost to businesses exceeded $50 billion.

Clever thieves can easily access an individual's personal and financial information. Seniors are among the easiest and financially well off targets for identity thieves. Many of the elderly live alone, or isolated away from family members. This isolation makes people vulnerable; under those circumstances, seniors are more likely to let a stranger have access to personal financial or identity information simply as a response to their kindness and time spent with the senior.

Because seniors are more likely to own their own home, have a good credit rating, have adequate savings and investments and receive regular pension or Social Security checks, they a much more valuable target than the average person. For seniors on the lower end of the economic scale, living on a fixed income or limited budget tempts them to look for quick cash or "new, secret" investments that will bring more profit to them than most investment channels. Many times, their entire retirement is emptied and their credit is ruined before they realize they have been taken.

Phony Cops Catching Criminal Bank Teller

This is a fairly new scam. The mark is contacted by someone claiming to be a member of the law enforcement community. The "law enforcement officer" informed them that they believe an employee at the local bank has been stealing from the bank and customers. They enlist the aide of the individual, ask them to go to bank, withdraw a large sum of money. The individual is instructed to then hand off the cash to the "law enforcement official", who will take the money back to their headquarters to verify the amount. In the end, the mark never hears from the again.

Splitting a Bag of Cash 3 Ways

Individuals are approached by 2 people who are supposedly strangers. They inform their new found friend that they "found" a bag of cash in the parking lot. One suggests they turn in it, and the other protests against that idea. They suggest that each of the three people go to their bank, withdraw $5,000 and place it in the bag. The money will then be split three ways. The money is then split three ways, but the scam artists split it in such a way that the mark is cheated out of a substantial portion of their investment.

Engine Trouble

This scam begins with an innocent trip to the grocery store. As soon as the senior exits their car and enters the store, the scammer goes to work. He or she approaches the car and finds some way to disable the vehicle, typically by detaching a spark-plug wire. The scammer then sits nearby & waits for the senior to return. When the car doesn't start, the con artist poses as a helpful passerby, fixes the car, and then demands a large cash reward. They are so bold many will demand to ride with the senior to a bank to get the money if they don't have enough money on them.

Credit Card Skimmers

Credit Card Skimmers are electronic devices that are placed on gasoline pumps. They steal the electronic information from the credit cards of people who use that pump. These scam artists can actually download this information wirelessly and leave the skimmer in place. Many gasoline stations use precautionary measures to protect their pumps. Ask your local station what they do to prevent this kind of scam.

Car Sliders

Watch out for "sliders", Sliders watch and wait patiently for women to pull up to a gasoline pump. While the individual is occupied with pumping gas, the driver thief will his car alongside the parked car getting gas, with his passenger side door next to the passenger door of the car getting gasoline. His accomplice quickly slides out of his seat, slides into the parked car and steals a purse or whatever else is close and has value. He then slides out of the victim's car and back into his own car for a quick escape.

Car Hopper Thieves

Car Hoppers make a game out of theft. They will get a group of people together, and hit a large neighborhood. The group members are given a set time limit to travel through the neighborhood, opening as many cars as possible, and taking whatever they can find. Then the group comes back together to compare their stolen goods with those of their friends.

Franchises

A tough economy pushes many seniors to look for ways to supplement their income. Some times that comes as the respond to the glut of seminars and infomercials that fill the airwaves, promising significant income through part-time or full time business. The world is full of great business  a opportunities and legitimate franchises that can help seniors earn an honest living, None of these opportunities are easy or inexpensive, and they all require time, sacrifice and effort, unlike the promises of instant wealth with no effort that many scams promise. Sadly enough, many seniors will empty their nest egg, only to find out too late that they have fallen prey to wolves in sheep's clothing.

There is a federal rule that may require specific information about business opportunities be given to potential buyers at least 10 days before any legal commitment or payments are made to a purchase any business opportunity or franchise. If the seller doesn't offer a disclosure document containing the following information, it should be a warning sign.

Disclosure documents should be requested, and if they still are not offered, the deal should not proceed. It's called the Franchise and Business Opportunity Rule (16 C.F.R. Part 436), and it is the Federal Trade Commission that it enforces. That information should include:

➢ The cost of starting and maintaining the franchise;

➢ The names, addresses and telephone numbers of at least 10 previous purchasers living closest to you;

- ➤ Information regarding the background and experience of the business' key executives;

- ➤ A financial statement of the seller that has been audited;

- ➤ A comprehensive list of the responsibilities the seller and purchaser will have to each other once the purchase is completed.

Call toll-free helpline to 1-877-FTC-HELP (382-4357) to verify the explanation with an attorney, a business advisor or the FTC. Even if there is not a legal requirement to provide a disclosure document in this instance, request one for your own information anyway.

The FTC offers some critical tips for consideration in avoiding being scammed with a franchise or business opportunity:

- ➤ Study the disclosure document and proposed contract carefully.

- ➤ Interview current owners in person.

- ➤ Don't rely on a list of references selected by the company because it may contain shills.

- ➤ Ask owners and operators how the information in the disclosure document matches their experiences with the company.

- ➤ Investigate claims about your potential earnings. Be suspicious of any company that does not show you in writing how it computed its earnings claims.

- ➤ Sellers also must tell you in writing the number and percentage of owners who have done as well as they claim you will.

- ➤ Recognize that once you buy the business, you may be competing with franchise owners or independent business people with more experience than you.

➢ **Shop around. Compare franchises with other business opportunities. Some companies may offer benefits not available from the first company you considered. The Franchise Opportunities Handbook, published annually by the U.S. Department of Commerce, describes more than 1,400 companies that offer franchises. Contact those that interest you. Request their disclosure documents and compare their offerings.**

➢ **Listen carefully to the sales presentation. Some sales tactics should signal caution. For example, if you are pressured to sign immediately "because prices will go up tomorrow," or "another buyer wants this deal," slow down. Be wary if the salesperson makes the job sound too easy. The thought of "easy money" may be appealing, but success generally requires hard work.**

➢ **Get the seller's promises in writing.**

Consider getting professional advice before you invest. Ask a lawyer, accountant or business advisor to read the disclosure document and proposed contract.

ONLINE SCAMS

Fake Antivirus

Computer users unwittingly download and install malware disguised as antivirus software, by following the messages which appear on their screen. The software then pretends to find multiple viruses on the victim's computer, "removes" a few, and asks for payment in order to take care of the rest. They are then linked to con artists' websites, professionally designed to make their bogus software appear legitimate, where they must pay a fee to download the "full version" of their "antivirus software".

Phishing

A modern scam in which the artist communicates with the mark, masquerading as a representative of an official organization with which the mark is doing business, in order to extract personal information which can then be used, for example, to steal money.

In a typical instance, the artist sends the mark an email pretending to be from a company, such as eBay. It is formatted exactly like email from that business, and will ask the mark to "verify" some personal information at the website, to which a link is provided, in order to "reactivate" his blocked account. The website is fake but designed to look exactly like the business' website. The site contains a form asking for personal information such as credit card numbers, which the mark feels compelled to give or lose all access to the service. When the mark submits the form (without double-checking the website address), the information is sent to the swindler. It can also be used with a random dialer computer or auto-dialer to get Social

Security number and birthdays from elderly patients recently released from the hospital. The auto-dialer call states it's from a reputable hospital or a pharmacy and message explains the need to "update records" to be from the hospital or a pharmacy.

Other online scams include advance-fee fraud, bidding fee schemes, click fraud, domain slamming, various spoofing attacks, web-cramming, and online versions of employment scams, romance scams, and fake rewards.

Fake Support Call

Unsuspecting computer owners and users are being targeted by people claiming to be from Windows i.e. Microsoft or from their internet provider and then telling them that their computer/machine is creating errors and they need to correct the faults on their computers, they even get people to go to one site or another to show them so called errors, they are then required to give their credit card details so that they can purchase some form of support then they are asked to allow remote connection so that they can fix the problems. The victim's computer is then infected with malware or spyware or remote connection software such as Virtualpcsecure. Microsoft has released this response however it seems the scams still continue.

Counterfeit Products

From designer clothing & purses to medication and medical products, knock offs can take many forms. Illegally duplicated movies and music are among the staples of the counterfeit items. When shopping online, it is not unusual for bargain hunting seniors to stumble across counterfeit or pirated goods.

Counterfeiters make a killing off of copied clothing, accessories, music, movies and a variety of tickets.

Consumers should avoid online purchases that don't have a solid reputation. Goods without warranties or "use-by dates" also should be viewed as highly suspect. Simple things like paying attention to spelling, confusing or misleading web addresses could be warning signals that the products offered may not be genuine.

Legitimate online retailers also encrypt their transactions with their customers. If a website does not encrypt its connections, you should probably choose to not transmit your personal information, including credit card numbers over that website. Look for a padlock icon on your Web browser; if it's there, then the data is encrypted. If there's not a padlock icon, you risk having your information stolen and abused.

Here are some basic tips when purchasing goods over the Internet:

➢ Primarily order from companies either you or someone you trust has previously dealt with or that you know to be legitimate. Discover whether or not there is a customer service number that you can contact should any problems arise.

➢ Do not provide any more personal information than is required. Unless you are absolutely certain the site is legitimate, never give out your Social Security number or driver's license number. If someone online asks you to reveal your passwords or any information used to install your online service then shut down the transaction immediately and don't return.

➢ Research the cost of shipping and handling fees for any items ordered. Don't let the seller choose for you, and don't assume they would pick the least expensive or best option for you.

➢ By federal law, sellers must ship items by the date they promise, or, if no delivery date is stated, within thirty 30 days after the order date. That being so, check the ship date when you order. If the seller is unable to ship the item within that time, they are required to notify you, or give you the option to cancel the order, and if so to send you a total refund.

➢ Research their website, or ask for the company's refund policy in writing.

➢ **Pay with a credit card, NOT with a debit card. If your item fails to arrive or if you believe you've been scammed, credit card companies will allow you to dispute the charge. With a debit card, the money is simply gone, and you may have compromised your entire checking account. Federal law protects you if someone uses your credit card, not your debit card, in an unauthorized fashion. Never, ever provide your checking account number.**

➢ **Keep a record of your purchase. If ordering online, print out a copy of your order form or any confirmation you receive.**

Online auctions are an easy place to get scammed. Even though sites like PayPal can protect your private information and allow you to pay safely, it doesn't protect buyers from being scammed with faulty or phony products.

Check out the ranking of online auctioneers, and contact your local Better Business Bureau to see if the company has complaints other buyers have lodged against it.

IRS IMPOSTOR PHONE SCAM

Crooks posing as IRS agents call the elderly, and using the last four numbers of the seniors Social Security Number, they seem believable over the phone. During one phase of this scam, over 20,000 taxpayers were contacted and swindled using this sophisticated scam, paying over $1 million to criminals posing as IRS agents.

The scam works like this... the phony IRS agent confronts the senior through the phone, many times using "spoofing" software to falsely display the 1-800 toll free number to the IRS, giving them even more credibility. During the call, they claim the senior owes a significant amount in back taxes, penalty and interest. Then they demand immediate payment using either a wire transfer or a pre-paid debit card. Should the victim argue or disagree with the "agent", they are threatened with more fines, loss of property or business, even jail time.

Follow up is critical to this scam. These clever crooks will create web domains that include use of IRS somewhere in the name, and email their victims from these email addresses. They will include very official sounding titles, badge numbers and even logos copied from the IRS website and pasted into their phony email. Keep an eye out for these signs that it might be an IRS Scam

IRS Contacts by Mail

The first key to spotting this scam is simple. The IRS first contacts people by mail about unpaid taxes rather than by phone or email.

IRS Payment Methods

Next, the IRS doesn't ask for payment using a pre-paid debit card or wire transfer.

IRS Lets You Call Them Back

The IRS won't be offended or disagree if you ask if you can call them back at the official IRS toll free number; scammers will argue and want you to stay on the line with them. If you think you may owe taxes, call the IRS at 800-829-1040. Legitimate IRS employees can verify if there really is a payment issue.

If you know you don't owe taxes or have no reason to think that you owe any taxes (for example, you've never received a bill or the caller made some bogus threats as described above), then report the incident to the Treasury

Inspector General for Tax Administration at 800-366-4484.

FINANCIAL EXPLOITATION BY RELATIVES & CAREGIVERS

Although this was mentioned earlier, it is significant enough to explain further. Caregivers, friends and relatives operate from a position of trust and relationship with the seniors, unlike strangers who would try to scam them. If ANY person takes, steals, keeps, withholds, or abuses the property, money, credit cards or property for personal gain, then it's a crime. There are many ways to do this, but among the most common are:

> ➢ cashing and stealing any pension or social security or retirement checks, without the permission of the senior;

> ➢ taking cash, checks or other valuables;

➢ refusing or withholding medical care or other services to keep the seniors money that was supposed to be spent for those purposes;

➢ Bullying, coercing or forcing the senior in any way to give up their money, property or resources.

➢ gifting or selling property that belongs to the senior, and doing so without their approval;

➢ using the debit or credit cards belonging to the senior without their permission;;

➢ borrowing money or property, and failing to return it;

➢ giving away any or all of the senior's money, even if it is to family members of the senior;

Close friends and family are not beyond using tactics like intimidation, emotional manipulation, deceit, false promises, coercion, blackmail or outright lies. To increase their chances of succeeding with their scam, they may try to isolate the senior from family, friends and other trusted parties, even to the point of convincing the unsuspecting senior that no one else actually really cares for them. This allows them to develop their plan without interference by others who might see through their schemes, and then either persuade or prevent the senior from giving into the scam.

Some caregivers or relatives will take advantage in a variety of other ways. Those include:

Deed or Title Transfer

A senior can be convinced that for "safety" or "tax savings" reasons, it's in their best interest to transfer ownership of property such as homes, real estate, or cars to the "trusted friend or family member." These scammers are not beyond using force, intimidation, simply overwhelming the senior with guilt, shame or fear to push them into making the transaction.

Joint Bank Accounts

Once the offender has convinced the elderly person that he or she needs help with his or her financial affairs, they convince them to add the offender the bank accounts. This gives the thief the ability to withdraw or transfer funds. Many of these kinds of criminals simply take advantage of the senior's limited capacity to make a wise or safe financial decision, and push them using fear and coercion.

Living Wills and Trusts

Many seniors worry about expensive probate fees and estate taxes will eat up the estate they wish to leave behind for loved ones. An individual can legally move property and assets into a trust. The challenge to this plan comes if the other individuals with access to the trust are themselves not trustworthy. A criminal family member or friend may persuade a senior to change their will, making the trickster the primary or sole beneficiary upon the senior's death.

It can be confusing and frustrating for seniors to figure out who is truly trustworthy, especially if there has been conflict or problems within a family. Any time there is are legal decisions being made regarding the assets of a senior, there truly is safety in numbers. Make sure there is a fair balance of family, friends and outside legal help who are aware of the senior's financial situation before final decisions are made. There is no guarantee that everyone will be happy with all decisions, but this can limit their exposure to being scammed.

Power Of Attorney and Durable Power Of Attorney

A Power of Attorney or Durable POA gives a person the legal authority to manage the elder's affairs, including their financial affairs, on the elder's behalf. This can be tremendously helpful to many seniors... unless it's abused. Honest people can help seniors make decisions that are in the elderly person's best interest. Abuse happens when the elder is tricked or pressured to sign the document; and then they make decisions or transactions that benefit themselves, to the detriment of the senior.

MEDICARE DRUG SCAMS: REMEMBER THESE WORDS!

Authentic

Stick with sources that have the best reputations, like AARP at http://www.aarp.org/medicarerx and Medicare at http://www.medicare.gov or (800) 633-4227.

Free

You should never, ever, never, never, ever, ever pay a fee to enroll in a Medicare drug plan.

Patience

This could be the most important point of all. NEVER allow anyone to pressure you or a loved one to rush their decision regarding

Medicare drug plans.

Phoney
Signing up for a drug plan over the phone with someone you've never met greatly increases the chance that you will be the victim of a scam.

File
Do it. Don't be ashamed, embarrassed or afraid. If you've been scammed regarding a Medicare drug plan, all law enforcement immediately... or sooner.

Refuse
If asked for any of your most important personal information, like your Social Security Number, Medicare ID #, bank accounts or credit card numbers.

Company

Your friends and family have your best interest at heart, and may see or sense things you wouldn't. Never meet alone with someone trying to sign you up for a Medicare plan, but instead take someone you trust with you.

Shut

Close the door on strange salesmen who come to your house. Although some may be honest and above board, a large number of these modern day "medicine men" are con artists scheming to take advantage of seniors. Seek support from law enforcement if they persist.

Inter-Not

It's just not safe to purchase plans or make payments on the internet. It's ok to enroll online as long as it's a legitimate site.

Cynical

If salesmen pitch the "it won't cost you a dime" line, then run the other way. Only in rare circumstances would plans not include the normal deductibles, co-pays and premiums that all insurance plans carry with them.

Smell

Many people who have been victims of a scam later say, "I knew something just seemed 'off' about the whole deal." Learn to trust your gut, and make any plan pass your own "smell" test.

BBB

AAA will come to your rescue if your car is in trouble. BBB is the Better Business Bureau, & they can do the same for you if you call them before you sign the dotted line on any Medicare Drug plan. Check out the name of

the company and individual. You may find
information that saves you tons of money.

*The following scams are not as common as those
just described, but are still practiced in various
forms and seniors should be cautious.*

"GET RICH QUICK" SCHEMES

"Get rich quick" schemes are extremely varied; these include fake franchises, real estate "sure things", instant riches books, wealth-building seminars, self-help gurus, sure-fire inventions, useless products, chain letters, fortune tellers, quack doctors, miracle pharmaceuticals, foreign exchange fraud, Nigerian money scams, charms and talismans. Variations include the pyramid scheme, the Ponzi scheme, and the Matrix sale.

Count Victor Lustig sold the "money-printing machine" which he claimed could copy $100 bills. The client, sensing huge profits, would buy the machines for a high price (usually over $30,000). Over the next twelve hours, the machine would produce just two more $100 bills, but after that it produced only blank paper, as its supply of hidden $100 bills would have become exhausted. By the time the clients realized that they had been scammed, Lustig was long gone. This type of scheme is also called the "money box" scheme.

Salting

Salting or "salting the mine" are terms for a scam in which gemstones or gold ore are planted in a mine or on the landscape, duping the greedy mark into purchasing shares in a worthless or non-existent mining company. During gold rushes, scammers would load shotguns with gold dust and shoot into the sides of the mine to give the appearance of a rich ore, thus "salting the mine".

Spanish Prisoner

The Spanish Prisoner scam—and its modern variant, the advance-fee fraud or "Nigerian scam"—take advantage of the victim's greed.

The basic premise involves enlisting the mark to aid in retrieving some stolen money from its hiding place. The victim sometimes believes he can cheat the con artists out of their money, but anyone trying this has already fallen for the essential con by believing that the money is there to steal (see also Black money scam). Note that the classic Spanish Prisoner trick also contains an element of the romance scam (see below).

Many con men employ extra tricks to keep the victim from going to the police. A common ploy of investment scammers is to encourage a mark to use money concealed from tax authorities. The mark cannot go to the authorities without revealing that he has committed tax fraud. Many swindles involve a minor element of crime or some other misdeed. The mark is made to think that he will gain money by helping fraudsters get huge sums out of a country (the classic advance-fee fraud/Nigerian scam); hence a mark cannot go to the police without revealing that he planned to commit a crime himself.

In a twist on the Nigerian fraud scheme, the mark is told he is helping someone overseas collect debts from corporate clients. Large checks stolen from businesses are mailed to the mark. These checks are altered to reflect the mark's name, and the mark is then asked to cash them and transfer all but a percentage of the funds (his commission) to the con artist. The checks are often completely genuine, except that the "pay to" information has been expertly changed. This exposes the mark not only to enormous debt when the bank reclaims the money from his account, but also to criminal charges for money laundering. A more modern variation is to use laser-printed counterfeit checks with the proper bank account numbers and payer information.

PERSUASION TRICKS

Persuasion fraud, when fraudsters persuade people only to target their money, is an old-fashioned type of fraud. We've already mentioned two of the most notable Persuasion Scams, the Grandparent Scam and the Romance Scam.

Fortune-Telling Fraud

One traditional swindle involves fortune telling. In this scam, a fortune teller uses his or her cold reading skill to detect that a client is genuinely troubled rather than merely seeking entertainment; or is a gambler complaining of bad luck. The fortune teller informs the mark that he is the victim of a curse, and that for a fee a spell can be cast to remove the curse. In Romany, this trick is called bujo ("bag") after one traditional format: the mark is told that the curse is in his money; he brings money in a bag to have the spell cast over it, and leaves with a bag of worthless paper. Fear of this scam has been one justification for legislation that makes fortune telling a crime.

This scam got a new lease on life in the electronic age with the virus hoax. Fake anti-virus software falsely claims that a computer is infected with viruses, and renders the machine inoperable with bogus warnings unless blackmail is paid. In the Datalink Computer Services incident, a mark was fleeced of several million dollars by a firm that claimed that his computer was infected with viruses, and that the infection indicated an elaborate conspiracy against him on the Internet.

GOLD BRICK SCAMS

Gold brick scams involve selling a tangible item for more than it is worth; they are named after selling the victim an allegedly golden ingot which turns out to be gold-coated lead.

Pig-In-A-Poke (Cat in a Bag)

Pig-in-a-poke originated in the late Middle Ages. The con entails a sale of a (suckling) "pig" in a "poke" (bag). The bag ostensibly contains a live healthy little pig, but actually contains a cat (not particularly prized as a source of meat). If one buys the bag without looking inside it, the person has bought something of less value than was assumed, and has learned first-hand the lesson caveat emptor.

"Buying a pig in a poke" has become a colloquial expression in many European languages, including English, for when someone buys something without examining it beforehand. In Slovenia, Croatia, Serbia, Bosnia and Herzegovina, Montenegro, Poland, Denmark, France, Belgium, Lithuania, Latvia, the Netherlands, Norway, Israel, Germany, Russia and Ukraine, the "pig" in the phrase is replaced by "cat", referring to the bag's actual content, but the saying is otherwise identical.

This is also said to be where the phrase "letting the cat out of the bag" comes from, although there may be other explanations. In Portugal, Brazil and other Portuguese speaking countries the "pig" in the phrase is replaced by a hare or jackrabbit. Therefore a victim thinks he is buying a hare, when in reality he is buying a cat, hence the expression "gato por lebre".

Thai Gems

The Thai gem scam involves layers of con men and helpers who tell a tourist in Bangkok of an opportunity to earn money by buying duty-free jewelry and having it shipped back to the tourist's home country. The mark is driven around the city in a tuk-tuk operated by one of the con men, who ensures that the mark meets one helper after another, until the mark is persuaded to buy the jewelry from a store also operated by the swindlers. The gems are real but significantly overpriced. This scam has been operating for 20 years in Bangkok, and is said to be protected by Thai police and politicians. A similar scam usually runs in parallel for custom-made suits. Many tourists are hit by con men touting both goods.

White-Van Speakers

In the white van speaker scam, low-quality loudspeakers are sold—stereotypically from a white van—as expensive units that have been greatly discounted. The salesmen explain the ultra-low price in a number of ways; for instance, that their employer is unaware of having ordered too many speakers, so they are sneakily selling the excess behind the boss's back. The "speaker men" are ready to be haggled down to a seemingly minuscule price, because the speakers they are selling, while usually functional, actually cost only a tiny fraction of their "list price" to manufacture.

The scam may extend to the creation of Web sites for the bogus brand, which usually sounds similar to that of a respected loudspeaker company. They will often place an ad for the speakers in the "For sale" Classifieds

152

of the local newspaper, at the exorbitant price, and then show you a copy of this ad to "verify" their worth.

People shopping for bootleg software, illegal pornographic images, bootleg music, drugs, firearms or other forbidden or controlled goods may be legally hindered from reporting swindles to the police. An example is the "big screen TV in the back of the truck": the TV is touted as "hot" (stolen), so it will be sold for a very low price. The TV is in fact defective or broken; it may in fact not even be a television at all, since some scammers have discovered that a suitably decorated oven door will suffice. The buyer has no legal recourse without admitting to the attempted purchase of stolen goods. This con is also known as "The Murphy Game".

EXTORTION/FALSE-INJURY TRICKS

Badger Game

The badger game extortion is often perpetrated on married men. The mark is deliberately coerced into a compromising position, a supposed affair for example, then threatened with public exposure of his acts unless blackmail money is paid.

Bogus Dry-Cleaning Bill Scam

A mail fraud typically perpetrated on local restaurateurs, this scheme takes a receipt from a legitimate dry cleaner in the target city, duplicates it thousands of times, and sends it to every upscale eatery in town. An attached note claims a server in the victim's restaurant spilled food, coffee, wine or salad dressing on a diner's expensive suit of clothes and demands reimbursement for dry cleaning costs. As the amount fraudulently claimed from each victim is relatively low, some will give the scammers the benefit of the doubt.

The scam's return address is a drop box; the rest of the contact information is fictional or belongs to an innocent third party. The original dry cleaning shop, which has nothing to do with the scheme, receives multiple irate enquiries from victimized restaurateurs.

Clip Joint

A clip joint or fleshpot is an establishment, usually a strip club or entertainment bar, typically one claiming to offer adult entertainment or bottle service, in which customers are tricked into paying money and receive poor, or no, goods or services in return. Typically, clip joints suggest the possibility of sex, charge excessively high prices for watered-down drinks, and then eject customers when they become unwilling or unable to spend more money. The product or service may be illicit, offering the victim no recourse through official or legal channels.

Coin-Matching Game

Also called a coin smack or smack game, two operators trick a victim during a game where coins are matched. One operator begins the game with the victim, then the second joins in. When the second operator leaves briefly, the first colludes with the victim to cheat the second operator. After rejoining the game, the second operator, angry at "losing," threatens to call the police. The first operator convinces the victim to pitch in hush money, which the two operators later split.

Insurance Fraud

Insurance fraud includes a wide variety of schemes in which the insured attempt to defraud their own insurance carriers, but when the victim is a private individual, the con artist tricks the mark into damaging, for example, the con artist's car, or injuring the con artist, in a manner that the con artist can later exaggerate.

One relatively common scheme involves two cars, one for the con artist, and the other for the shill. The con artist will pull in front of the victim, and the shill will pull in front of the con artist before slowing down. The con artist will then slam on his brakes to "avoid" the shill, causing the victim to rear-end the con artist. The shill will accelerate away, leaving the scene. The con artist will then claim various exaggerated injuries in an attempt to collect from the victim's insurance carrier despite having intentionally caused the accident.

Insurance carriers, who must spend money to fight even those claims they believe are fraudulent, frequently pay out thousands of dollars—a tiny amount to the carrier despite being a significant amount to an individual—to settle these claims instead of going to court.

A variation of this scam occurs in countries where insurance premiums are generally tied to a Bonus-Malus rating: the con artist will offer to avoid an insurance claim, settling instead for cash compensation. Thus, the con artist is able to evade a professional damage assessment, and get an untraceable payment in exchange for sparing the mark the expenses of a lowered merit class.

GAMBLING TRICKS

Fiddle Game

The fiddle game uses the pigeon drop technique. A pair of con men work together, one going into an expensive restaurant in shabby clothes, eating, and claiming to have left his wallet at home, which is nearby. As collateral, the con man leaves his only worldly possession, the violin that provides his livelihood.

After he leaves, the second con man swoops in, offers an outrageously large amount (for example $50,000) for such a rare instrument, then looks at his watch and runs off to an appointment, leaving his card for the mark to call him when the fiddle-owner returns.

The mark's greed comes into play when the "poor man" comes back, having gotten the money to pay for his meal and redeem his violin. The mark, thinking he has an offer on the table, then buys the violin from the fiddle player who "reluctantly" agrees to sell it for a certain amount that still allows the mark to make a "profit" from the valuable violin. The result is the two con men are richer (less the cost of the violin), and the mark is left with a cheap instrument.

Glim-Dropper

The glim-dropper scam requires several accomplices, one of whom must be a one-eyed man. One grifter goes into a store and pretends he has lost his glass eye. Everyone looks around, but the eye cannot be found. He declares that he will pay a thousand-dollar reward for the return of his eye, leaving contact information.

The next day, an accomplice enters the store and pretends to find the eye. The storekeeper (who is in on it), pretends to think about the reward & offers to take the eye and return it to its owner. The finder insists he will return it himself, and demands the owner's address. Thinking he will lose all chance of the reward, the storekeeper offers a hundred dollars for the eye. The finder bargains him up to $250, and departs. The one-eyed man, of course, cannot be found and does not return.

Lottery Fraud by Proxy

Lottery fraud by proxy is a scam in which the scammer buys a lottery ticket with old winning numbers. He or she then alters the date on the ticket so that it appears to be from the day before, and therefore a winning ticket. He or she then sells the ticket to the mark, claiming it is a winning ticket, but for some reason, he or she is unable to collect the prize (not eligible, etc.). The particular cruelty in this scam is that if the mark attempts to collect the prize, the fraudulently altered ticket will be discovered and the mark held criminally liable.

Three-Card Monte

Three-card Monte, "find the queen", the "three-card trick", or "follow the lady" is essentially the same as the centuries-older shell game or thimblerig (except for the props). The trickster shows three playing cards to the audience, one of which is a queen (the "lady"), then places the cards face-down, shuffles them around, and invites the audience to bet on which

one is the queen. At first the audience is skeptical, so the shill places a bet, and the scammer allows him to win. In one variation of the game, the shill will (apparently surreptitiously) peek at the lady, ensuring that the mark also sees the card. This is sometimes enough to entice the audience to place bets, but the trickster uses sleight of hand to ensure that he always loses, unless the con man decides to let him win, hoping to lure him into betting much more. The mark loses whenever the dealer chooses to make him lose.

A variation on this scam exists in Barcelona, Spain, but with the addition of a pickpocket. The dealer and shill behave in an overtly obvious manner, attracting a larger audience. When the pickpocket succeeds in stealing from a member of the audience, he signals the dealer. The dealer then shouts the word "aguas"—colloquial for "Watch Out!"—and the three split up. The audience is left believing that the police are coming, and that the performance was a failed scam.

A variant of this scam exists in Mumbai, India. The shill says loudly to the dealer that his cards are fake and that he wants to see them. He takes the card and folds a corner and says in a hushed voice to the audience that he has marked the card. He places a bet and wins. Then he asks the others to place bets as well. When one of the audience bets a large sum of money, the cards are switched.

Who's Who Scam

Operators of fraudulent "Who's Who" directories would offer listings or "membership" to purchasers who are often unaware of the low rates the directories in question are consulted.

Diploma Mill

Governmental bodies maintain a list of entities which accredit educational institutions. The US Department of Education, for instance, oversees higher education accreditation in the United States.

Most diploma mills are not accredited by such an entity, although many obtain accreditation from other organizations (such as accreditation mills or corrupt foreign officials) to appear legitimate. Graduates of these institutions risk that the qualifications gained at these institutions may not be sufficient for further study, lawful employment or professional licensure as their issuers do not hold locally-valid accreditation to grant the degrees.

Some diploma mills perform no instruction or examination, instead issuing credentials based on payment and "life experience". A few have unknowingly issued degrees and credentials to animals.

World Luxury Association

The World Luxury Association is a self-proclaimed international organization based in China that offers "official registration" for luxury brands, and inclusion in an "official list" of luxury brands, in return for a fee.

OTHER CONS, TRICKS & SCAMS

Art Student

The art student scam is common in major Chinese cities. A small group of 'students' will start a conversation, claiming that they want to practice their English. After a short time they will change the topic to education and will claim that they are art students and they want to take you to a free exhibition.

The exhibition will usually be in a small, well hidden rented office and the students will show you some pieces which they claim to be their own work and will try to sell them at a high price, despite the pieces usually being nothing more than an internet printout worth a fraction of their asking price. They will often try 'guilt tricks' on people who try to bargain the price.

Big Store

The Big Store is a technique for selling the legitimacy of a scam and typically involves a large team of con artists and elaborate sets. Often a building is rented and furnished as a legitimate and substantial business. The "betting parlor" setup in The Sting is an example.

Change Raising

Change raising, also known as a quick-change artist, is a common short con and involves an offer to change an amount of money with someone, while at the same time taking change or bills back and forth to confuse the person as to how much money is actually being changed.

For example, a con artist shopping at a gas station pays for a cheap item (under a dollar) and gives the clerk a ten dollar bill. The con gets back nine ones and the change and then tells the clerk he has a one and will exchange ten ones for a ten. Here's the con: get the clerk to hand over the $10 BEFORE handing over the ones. Then the con hands over nine ones and the $10. The clerk will assume a mistake and offer to swap the ten for a one. Then the con will probably just say: "Here's another one, give me a $20 and we're even." Notice that the con just swapped $10 for $20. The $10 was the store's money, not the cons.

To avoid this con, keep each transaction separate and never ever permit the customer to handle the original ten before handing over the ten ones. Another variation is to flash a $20 bill to the clerk, then ask for something behind the counter. When the clerk turns away, the con artist can swap the bill he is holding to a lesser bill. The clerk might then make change for the larger bill, without noticing it has been swapped. The technique works better when bills are the same color at a glance like, for instance, U.S. dollar bills.

A similar technique exists when a con comes to a gas station with a young clerk, buying something cheap, showing him an uncommonly huge bill while not giving it and telling the clerk to prepare the change. While he's busy counting the change, the con would ask many questions in order to disturb the young clerk. When change is counted and ready the con is acting as if he had given the huge bill. If the clerk does not remember having received the bill, the con will say he gave him the money. If the clerk is weak or disturbed enough, he could let the con go away with the change.

Fake Casting Agent Scam

In this scam, the confidence artist poses as a casting agent for a modeling agency searching for new talent. The aspiring model is told that he will need a portfolio or comp card. The mark will pay an upfront fee to have photos and create his portfolio, after which he will be sent on his way in the hope that his agent will find him work in the following weeks. Of course, he never hears back from the confidence artist.

In a variation on this scam, the confidence artist is a casting agent involved with the adult entertainment industry. The mark is taken to the artist's office for an interview, in which she is told that she will have to pose for nude photos or shoot a casting video, usually involving sexual acts. Upon her agreement, the mark is sent on her way, as before. She may not have to pay upfront for a portfolio, but any material generated during her interview may be used and sold by the confidence artist without any payment to the mark.

Fraudulent Directory Solicitations

In this scam, tens of thousands of solicitations in the guise of an invoice are mailed to businesses nationwide.

They may contain a disclaimer such as "This is a solicitation for the order of goods or services, or both, and not a bill, invoice, or statement of account due. You are under no obligation to make any payments on account of this offer unless you accept this offer." (From 39 USC. 3001d2A) or 'THIS IS NOT A BILL. THIS IS A SOLICITATION. YOU ARE UNDER NO OBLIGATION TO PAY THE AMOUNT STATED ABOVE UNLESS YOU ACCEPT THIS OFFER.' (From USPS Domestic Mail Manual §CO31, Part 1.2) but are otherwise designed to appear to be invoices or renewals of existing display advertising in a trade directory or publication.

The correspondence is formatted like an invoice, often with a sequential identification number, date, personalized description of the information to be published, payment details and total amount due which includes a token discount if paid within a specified time period. In some cases, the company's current advertisement clipped from an existing publication (such as Thomas Register, Hotel and Travel Index or Official Meeting Facilities Guide) is attached to a solicitation for advertising in an unaffiliated, rival publication which operates from a drop box.

A similar scheme uses solicitations which appear to be invoices for local yellow pages listings or advertisements. As anyone can publish a yellow page directory, the promoted book is not the incumbent local exchange carrier's local printed directory but a rival, which may have limited distribution if it appears at all. Instead of clearly stating audited circulation, the solicitations will confusingly claim to "offer

50,000 copies" or claim "thousands of readers" without indicating whether the inferred quantity of directories was actually printed, let alone sold.

The intent is that a small fractional percentage of businesses either mistake the solicitations for invoices (paying them) or mistake them for a request for corrections and updates to an existing listing (a tactic to obtain a businessperson's signature on the document, which serves as a pretext to bill the victim).

Jam Auction

In this scam, the confidence artist poses as a retail sales promoter, representing a manufacturer, distributor, or set of stores. The scam requires assistants to manage the purchases/money exchanges while the pitchman keeps the energy level up. Passersby are enticed to gather and listen to a pitchman standing near a mass of appealing products. The trickster entices by referring to the high-end products, but claims to be following rules that he must start with smaller items. The small items are described, and 'sold' for a token dollar amount - with as many audience participants as are interested each receiving an item. The pitchman makes an emotional appeal such as saying "Raise your hand if you're happy with your purchase" and when hands are raised, directs his associates to return everyone's money (they keep the product). This exchange is repeated with items of increasing value to establish the expectation of a pattern.

Eventually, the pattern terminates by ending the 'auction' without reaching the high-value items, and stopping midway through a phase where the trickster retains the collected money from that round of purchases. Marks feel vaguely dissatisfied, but have goods in their possession, and the uplifting feeling of having demonstrated their own happiness several times. The marks do not realize that the total value of goods received is significantly less than the price paid in the final round. Auction/refund rounds may be interspersed with sales rounds that are not refunded, keeping marks off-balance and hopeful that the next round will refund. The Jam Auction has its roots in Carny culture.

Money Exchange

This scam occurs when exchanging foreign currency. If a large amount of cash is exchanged the victim will be told to hide the money away quickly before counting it ("You can't trust the locals"). A substantial amount will be missing.

In some cases, insisting on counting to make sure the money is all there is the basis for a clever scam. The scam is sometimes called the Santo Domingo Sting, after an incident that took place there in the early 1990s. It works in countries where only banks and other designated parties are allowed to hold and exchange the local currency for US dollars at an "official" rate that is significantly lower than the "street" rate. It also requires a greedy tourist who wants to beat the official rate by dealing with illegal money changers.

A person posing as an illegal money changer will approach the tourist with an offer to buy dollars at an illegal rate that may be even higher than the street rate. The changer offers to buy only large US currency, typically, a 100 dollar bill. As soon as the victim (the "mark") shows his $100 bill, the changer will actually count out and clearly show the promised amount of pesos. He then will push the pesos into the hands of the "mark" and urge they be counted as he takes the $100. "See, you've got the money. I'll wait while you make sure. Count it out loud so there is no mistake."

As the mark's careful count exceeds "street" rate, the changer pretends to realize he has overpaid the mark, and he becomes irrationally agitated and angry, accusing the mark of cheating. He grabs his money back, pushes the mark's bill back into his hands and takes back the pesos. The scam has been completed. The tourist has just lost $99. The mark has been handed back a pre-folded $1 bill that has been swapped for the mark's $100 bill while he was distracted counting the pesos. (US currency is largely uniform in size and color, meaning that when folded, a $1 and a $100 bill are almost indistinguishable.) The money changer's anger is a ruse to confuse the mark and delay his unfolding of the single bill until the scammer has departed.

<u>*Mystery Shopping*</u>

There is a fraudulent confidence trick (a form of advance fee fraud) perpetrated on people in several countries who wish to be mystery shoppers. A person is sent a money order, often from Western Union, or check for a larger sum than a mystery purchase he is required to make, with a request to deposit it into his bank account, use a portion for a mystery purchase and fee, and wire the remainder through a wire transfer company such as Western Union or MoneyGram; the money is to be wired immediately as response time is being evaluated. The check is fraudulent, and is returned unpaid by the victim's bank, after the money has been wired.

> *"Watch out for some online mystery shopping scams which will cost you money for either training or for signing up without the promise of any work."*

One scam involved fraudulent websites using a misspelled URL to advertise online and in newspapers under a legitimate company's name. It should be remembered that this is not the only type of mystery shopping scam taking place which involves money being paid, as it has been widely reported in the UK that shoppers should "Watch out for some online mystery shopping scams which will cost you money for either training or for signing up without the promise of any work."

Valid mystery shopping companies do not normally send their clients checks prior to work being completed, and their advertisements usually include a contact person and phone number. Some fraudulent checks can be identified by a financial professional.

On February 3, 2009, The Internet Crime Complaint Center issued a warning on this scam.

A legitimate company that occasionally sends prepayment for large transactions says "We do occasionally fund upfront for very large spend purchases but we use checks or direct bank transfers which should mean you can see when they are cleared and so can be sure you really do have the money."

It is standard practice for mystery shopping providers evaluating services such as airlines to arrange for the airfare to be issued beforehand at their own expenses (usually by means of a frequent flyer reward ticket). In any case, it is unlikely that any bona-fide provider would allocate a high-value assignment to a new shopper or proactively recruit new ones for that purpose, preferring instead to work with a pool of existing pre-vetted experienced shoppers.

Pigeon Drop

The pigeon drop, which is depicted early in the film The Sting, involves the mark or pigeon assisting an elderly, weak or infirm stranger to keep a large sum of money safe for him. In the process, the stranger (actually a confidence trickster) puts his money with the mark's money in an envelope or briefcase, with which the mark is then entrusted. The container is then switched for an identical one which contains no money, and a situation is engineered where the mark has the opportunity to escape with the money. If the mark takes this chance, he is merely fleeing from his own money, which the con artist will have kept or handed off to an accomplice.

Psychic Surgery

Psychic surgery is a con game in which the trickster uses sleight of hand to apparently remove malignant growths from the mark's body. A common form of medical fraud in underdeveloped countries, it imperils victims who may fail to seek competent medical attention.

Recovery Room

A recovery room scam is a form of advance-fee fraud where the scammer (sometimes posing as a law enforcement officer or attorney) calls investors who have been sold worthless shares (for example in a boiler-room scam), and offers to buy them, to allow the investors to recover their investments. The scam involves requiring an advance fee before the payment can take place, for example a "court fee".

Rip Deal

The Rip Deal is a swindle very popular in Europe and is essentially a pigeon drop confidence trick. In a typical variation scammers will target, say, a jeweler, and offer to buy some substantial amount of his wares at a large markup provided he perform some type of under-the-table cash deal, originally exchanging Swiss francs for euros. This exchange goes through flawlessly, at considerable profit for the mark. Sometime later the scammers approach the mark with a similar proposition, but for a larger amount of money (and thus a larger return for the mark). His confidence and greed inspired by the previous deal, the merchant agrees—only to have his money and goods taken, by sleight-of-hand or violence, at the point of exchange.

Wedding Planner Scam

Wedding planner scams prey on the vulnerability of young couples, during a time when they are most distracted and trusting, to embezzle funds for the planner's personal use. In the first type of fraud, the wedding planner company may offer a free wedding in a tie-up with a media station for a couple in need of charity, and collect the donations from the public that were meant for the wedding. In a second type of fraud, the planner asks couples to write checks to vendors (tents, food, and cakes) but leave the name field empty, which the planner promises to fill in. As most vendors were never hired nor paid, the scam would then be exposed on the day of the wedding. A real life example is a Kansas TV station story of a wedding planner, Caitlin Hershberger Theis, who scammed three couples through her wedding planner consultancy, Live, Love and be Married using these two schemes.

Blessing Scam

The blessing scam targets elderly Chinese immigrant women, convincing them that an evil spirit threatens their family and that this threat can be removed by a blessing ceremony involving a bag filled with their savings, jewelry or other valuables. During the ceremony, the con artists switch the bag of valuables with an identical bag with valueless contents and make off with the victim's cash or jewelry.

Travel

Compared with younger adults, seniors often have more leisure time and are attracted to low-cost travel packages. However, many of these packages cost far more than market rates, provide substandard accommodations, or do not provide the promised services.

Confidence Games

These frauds generally do not involve a product or service; instead, they include a broad array of deceitful scenarios to get cash from the elderly. The offender may pretend to be in a position of authority (e.g., a bank examiner), or otherwise trustworthy, concocting a story to get the victim to hand over cash, then disappearing. For example, the perpetrators of "lottery scams" claim to have won the lottery but to have no bank account in which to deposit the winnings. The offender promises the victim a premium in exchange for use of his or her account. After the victim makes a "good faith" payment to the offender, the victim never hears from the offender again.

Telemarketing

Offenders call people at home, using high-pressure tactics to solicit money for fraudulent investments, insurance policies, travel packages, charities, and sweepstakes. Fraudulent telemarketing operations are designed to limit the benefit to the customer while maximizing the profit for the telemarketer and for the highly efficient contact of a lot of potential customers.

Mail

Fraudulent prize and sweepstakes operations often mail materials to a wide audience, relying on potential victims to "self-select" by returning a postcard or calling to indicate their interest. The mailings often look official, use extensive personalization (e.g., repeating the recipient's name in the text), include claims of authenticity, have contradictory content or "double-talk," and make a seemingly low-key request for the recipient to submit a small fee.

Face-To-Face Contact

Some frauds involving products and services (e.g., home and auto repairs) require face-to-face contact at either the victim's home or a business. Alternatively, a scammer gains entry to the victim's home by posing as a utility worker and distracts the victim while an accomplice burglarizes the home.

Successful frauds share common elements. The offenders gain trust and confidence through their charisma, by using a business name similar to that of a well-established organization, or by communicating a concern for the elder's well-being. They create the impression that the elder has been "chosen" or is "lucky" to receive the offer, and that such offers are rare. They encourage their victims to make an immediate decision or commitment to purchase products or services, which effectively limits the opportunity for consultation with others.

Further, since the "special" offers are available to only a select group of customers, the offenders ask the victims to be discreet and not discuss the details, shrouding the transaction in secrecy and decreasing the chance of discovery by a family member, neighbor, or other concerned party. The frauds occur quickly, with little risk of exposure.

Odometer Fraud

Odometer fraud is the illegal practice of rolling back odometers to make it appear that a motor vehicle has lower mileage than it actually does. Any person who disconnects, resets, or alters the odometer on a motor vehicle with the intent to defraud a subsequent purchaser or lessee is in violation of federal law. See 49 U.S.C. 32701-32711. Penalties can include a civil fine of up to $2000 for each violation and imprisonment for up to three years. Violators may also be liable in a private lawsuit for three times the actual damages or $1500, whichever is greater.

Federal law requires that any person transferring ownership of a motor vehicle to provide the transferee a written disclosure of the cumulative mileage registered on the odometer OR IF THE ACTUAL MILEAGE IS UNKNOWN a disclosure to that effect. That disclosure is to be contained on the title issued in connection with each transfer.

The written disclosure must be signed by the transferor, including his printed name. The transferor must certify that to the best of his knowledge, the odometer reading reflects the actual mileage, or that the odometer reading reflects the amount of mileage in excess of the designed mechanical odometer limit. If the transferor knows that the odometer reading differs from the mileage, he must include a statement that the odometer reading does not reflect the actual mileage and should not be relied upon. In addition, the disclosure must contain the following information:

> The odometer reading at the time of the transfer (not including tenths of miles);

> The date of the transfer;

> The transferor's name and current address;

> The transferee's name and current address; and

➢ **The identity of the vehicle, including its make, model, year, and body type, and its vehicle identification number.**

The written disclosure must also refer to the Federal law and shall state that failure to complete or providing false information may result in fines and/or imprisonment.

POINTERS FOR A FRAUD-FREE VACATION

Empty Your Billfold

It's safer to only take the most essential items with you on vacation- a couple of different credit cards at most, and your driver's license for identification purposes. Once you get to your destination, lock one of your credit cards up, either in your hotel room, or a safe deposit alternative that many hotels offer. NEVER take your Social Security card with you, or your Medicare card either.

Call Your Credit Card Companies

Make a quick phone call to credit card companies for the cards you'll be taking with you, and inform them about your upcoming travels. It can not only prevent your card from being used back at home while you're not there, but it could also prevent your card from being shut off by a well meaning card company.

This happens when credit card companies see numerous purchases outside your normal geographic spending areas, or outside your normal spending habits. They assume that your credit card activity outside your normal spending locations is fraudulent, leaving you without access to your credit card by shutting it down in an effort to protect you. Let them know when, where and how long you'll be traveling.

Guard Your Personal Credit

You have the option to freeze your credit if you will be traveling for an extended period of time. It's simple enough to unfreeze the credit upon returning from the trip. It's very important that after you return that you closely examine your future credit card bills for possible fraudulent charges by dishonest waiters and shop owners who handled your credit card. It's advisable to run your credit report several months later at www.annualcreditreport.com to make sure no one has opened fraudulent accounts in your man.

SCAM PREVENTION WORKSHEET

The AARP has created a handy checklist to help you discern whether you're being scammed or not. It's not foolproof, but it's a great tool to use. Take plenty of notes, and if their answers set off any warning signals, or their failure to give adequate answers becomes obvious, exercise your right to hang up!

1. Note the date and time of the call... Is the call before 8: a.m. or after 9 p.m.?
Hang up if the answer is yes. All organizations that follow federal telemarketing guidelines must limit their calls to this 13-hour period.

2. Has the caller fully identified the organization that he/she represents immediately after you answer?
Ask for, and jot down, the full name, address, and phone number of the person making the call

and the organization(s) that the caller
represents.

3. **Does the caller work for the organization itself or for a fund-raising firm?**

Hang up if the caller hesitates to provide any of this information. Organizations that heed federal telemarketing guidelines should immediately identify themselves.

4. **Does the caller represent a charitable organization?**

What is the charitable purpose of the organization?

5. **Is it registered with the state (with the Secretary of State, state Department of Justice or Attorney General)?**

Legitimate businesses will be licensed and verifiable. If you're approached by one that is not, send them on their way.

6. **What percentage of its total income does the charity spend on its program?**

Don't settle for vague descriptions of the organization's activities that emphasize the problem without explaining what the charity is actually doing about it. Also, make sure that at least 50% to 60% of your donation will go toward actual charitable work---not fund-raising expenses.

7. **Is the caller offering a product, service or contest of some sort?**

How much does the product or service cost?

8. **Is the sale final or nonrefundable?**

Does the caller seek payment prior to delivering the product or services?

Hang up if the caller seeks payment prior to delivery of the product or service - or if the offer does not come with a money-back guarantee.

9. **Does the caller seek cash?**
Hang up immediately if the answer is yes. Legitimate organizations do not seek cash payments via the phone.

10. **Will the caller send details of the charity or products/service in writing - and therefore give you time to carefully review the offer?**
Hang up immediately if the answer is no – or if you must act "right away." Legitimate organizations will respect your interest in taking time to review offers prior to making a decision.

11. **If you think you have received a SCAM, please forward the ENTIRE email to Identify Theft Resource Center (ITRC) at: <u>itrc@idtheftcenter.org</u> and they will forward it to the FBI for you and let you know if it is a confirmed scam.**

To verify a suspected scam, the Identity Theft Resource Center recommends the following steps:

> Contact the company involved directly, using a customer service number you find in the phone book or that you have used in the past.

> THINK FIRST – ACT SECOND. The action to take is to verify a contact by the company before responding to the email. Do not even send a "do not contact me again."

> Contact the FBI at www.ifccfbi.gov or your local State Attorney General's office.

> Contact the Federal Trade Commission at 877-FTC HELP or send it via email to: http://spam@uce.gov

> Remember, URLs that begin with "http" are

not secure. Only those that begin "https" are secure sites for sending sensitive information.

➢ Avoid scams that appear to use telephone numbers in the U.S. but are expensive out-of-country numbers. If you're not sure where a telephone number is located, use this free Area Code Decoder: http://decoder.americom.com/cgi-bin/decoder.cg.

SCAM RISK SURVEY

	Question	Yes	No
1.	When a family member or friend is in the home, does the senior seem withdrawn, reluctant to talk, depressed or moody?		
2.	If the senior has a caregiver or home health provider, are they a private hire, not affiliated with a reputable firm?		
3.	Does the senior have a balanced skepticism of deals that are "too good to be true", and unrealistic advertising?		
4.	Is the senior visited less than once per month by family members and friends who they trust?		

5.	Is the senior unaware of where they can seek out help from law enforcement or consumer protection regarding scams?		
6.	Is the senior receiving their most important financial advice without consulting family or friends who will benefit from it financially?		
7.	Is the senior shy or hesitant about introducing family and friends to a new business or financial contact?		
8.	Does the senior have an increasing number of new products or services being provided in their home?		

9.	Is there a new influential person that has moved into the home or the life of the senior, and there is no logical reason for them to be there?		
10.	Has the potential scammer shown up in a negative light in a Google search, or with the Better Business Bureau?		
To total your points, award 10 points to every question that was answered YES.			
	TOTAL POINTS		
	0- 30 Points	*Great Shape, not very likely to be scammed.*	
	40- 60 Points	*Caution, may fall victim to a scam.*	
	70- 100 Points	*Warning!!! Likely to be scammed soon!*	

<u>REMEMBER THESE IMPORTANT FACTS!</u>

<u>Ask a Lot of Questions</u>

If there is a new person or company in the picture, then ask about them, and ask for details... ASK FOR LOTS OF DETAILS... You may not ultimately have any choice in whatever decisions are made, but awareness is the best tool available to limit damage from scams.

<u>Get a 2nd Opinion</u>

Entire life savings have been wiped out by "trusted advisors" who have taken charge of a senior's finances. Always encourage seniors to seek out a 2nd opinion as a way of offering a second set of eyes on a potential investment.

Have Regular Reviews

Ask for regular reviews of financial investments, quarterly if possible. This allows you to have a consistent base line, and provides regular accountability.

Report Criminal or Unethical Activity

The best way to prevent future scams is to report on those who perpetrate them, and assist in their prosecution any way possible. Encourage anyone who has been scammed to talk to law enforcement, and follow through with prosecution.

Do Your Own Research

Remind seniors that it's empty trust to believe that the government or other business entities have researched and cleared all telemarketing companies, home repair companies or financial planners.

Contact the Law When Necessary

Scammers and unscrupulous vendors will only be stopped from doing further damage if they are arrested and punished. For that to happen, victims of these crimes must put aside their shame, guilt or embarrassment and report these to law enforcement and to consumer protection agencies.

Hire & Use Trusted Companies
Resist the temptation to hire workers directly, outside the direction of the company they work for. In some instances this is a breach of contract for the employee or the individual. Regardless, the senior runs a significant risk since individual workers have no accountability, and may not be covered by necessary insurance.

HOLD ON TO YOUR MONEY, TO YOUR SAVINGS, & TO YOUR RETIREMENT!!!

IT'S YOURS!

TEN LAWS OF PROTECTION FOR SENIORS

Law of Pay to Play

When asked to purchase something for the chance to win, JUST SAY NO!

Law of No Numbers

Your personal info is the key to your financial life. If someone asks you for your account numbers or SSN over the phone, JUST SAY NO!

Law of Not Now

If challenged or pushed to sign any number of legal or financial documents, while discouraging you from getting a second opinion, JUST SAY NO!

Law of Second Opinions

Always seek the advice and perspective of financial and legal counsel when considering spending, investing or committing large sums of money. If pushed to press ahead without seeking such counsel, JUST SAY NO!

Law of Face to Face

Absolutely refuse to conduct business over the phone, unless you have gone to a website or your bill/paperwork, and initiated a call to them. If someone calls you and demands you do business during their call, JUST SAY NO!

Law of License Only

Do not hire home repair contractors, especially those offering to do repairs after a storm, unless they are local and offer you a verifiable copy of their license. JUST SAY NO!

Law of Pros Know

Secure your financial future by using a reputable elder estate attorney or financial planner. From anyone else who offers, JUST SAY NO!

Law of Show Me Your Badge

You don't owe it to anyone to let them into your home. Demand ID from anyone doing a home inspection. If they refuse, JUST SAY NO!

Law of No Fear

Don't be afraid of intimidation or speculation. If someone uses scare tactics about dangers in your home to get you to commit to repairs, JUST SAY NO!

Law of No Withdrawal

If someone wants you to withdraw large amounts of money for a purchase or any other reason, JUST SAY NO!

CONTACT INFORMATION

__National Fraud Information Center__
Phone: 1-800-876-7060

This is the best consumer resource for reporting telemarketing fraud and report suspicious activity on the Internet. Individuals may also submit complaints online. This is organization is a partnership of the National Association of Attorneys General and the Federal Trade Commission.

Complaints are taken, and information is entered in the NFIC database and referred to various federal and state regulatory and enforcement agencies: the FBI, Secret Service, U. S. Postal Inspectors, Securities and Exchange Commission, and U. S. Attorneys. Reports of suspected telemarketing or Internet fraud can easily be filed on line at

http://www.dora.state.co.us/pls/real/CCTS_oWE
B.trans_complaint_form.

Federal Trade Commission Consumer Response Center
CRC-240
Washington, DC 20580

Phone: Toll-free 1-877-FTC-HELP (382-4357) or
1-877-ID-THEFT (438-4338)

Chain Letters
Chain letters used to be much more prevalent than they are today, but they still circulate in a variety of forms even now. If you know a senior who you feel has fallen victim to a chain letter scam, have them send that information to:

United States Postal Inspection Service

Criminal Investigations Service Center

Attn: Mail Fraud

222 S Riverside Plaza   Suite 1250

Chicago, IL 60606-6100

There are three criteria for an illegal chain letter:
- ➢ **If the letter asks for money; OR**
- ➢ **If there is an element of misrepresentation; OR**
- ➢ **If the letter purports that you can expect to receive sums of money.**

Junk Mail

Mail Preference Service

Direct Marketing Association

1120 Avenue of the Americas

New York, NY 10036

Phone: (212) 768-7277

Fax: (212) 302-6714

Consumers can write to the Mail Preference Service to stop their name from being sold to most large mailing-list companies. This will not remove their name from any lists that already have their name. Consumers can write to any companies individually to have their name removed from their list.

Mail Fraud

U.S. Postal Inspection Service
1745 Stout Street, Suite 900
Denver, CO 80299-3034
Phone: (303) 313-5320
Toll-free: 1-800-372-8347
Fax: (303) 313-5351

The U.S. Postal Inspection Division handles complaints covering mail fraud. Seniors should be leery of any of offers received through the mail that sound too good to be true. Any sweepstakes, lotteries, or contests requiring cash up front are usually scams. A fantastic guide for spotting and protection against mail fraud is available on-line at http://www.usps.com/cpim/ftp/pubs/pub300a_print.htm.

Federal Law – CAN-SPAM Act of 2003

Congress passed the "Controlling the Assault of Non-Solicited Pornography and Marketing Act" ("CAN-SPAM Act") in 2003. It is designed to deal with spam & junk e-mail messages delivering either a commercial offer or pornographic images. CAN-SPAM Act prohibits transmission of any e-mail that contains false or misleading header (or "from" line) information and prohibits false or misleading "subject" line information.

This act also requires a functioning return e-mail address or similar mechanism for allowing the addressee to "opt out" of receiving any further messages from the sender. Senders must comply with any opt out requests within 10 business days. The FTC has primary authority to enforce CAN-SPAM Act, although state attorneys general and Internet Service providers also may enforce its provisions.

For more info on spam & junk e-mail can be found at

www.ftc.gov/bcp/menus/consumer/tech/spam.s htm

SOURCES

www.fbi.gov

www.wikipedia.org

www.ncoa.org

www.aarp.org

www.coloradoattorneygeneral.gov

www.amac.us

www.usa.gov

www.bbb.org

www.sec.gov

www.consumerfraudreporting.org/

www.epic.org

CPSIA information can be obtained at www.ICGtesting.com
Printed in the USA
LVOW11s1955190216

475863LV00001B/236/P